IN THE BEGINNING WAS THE WORD

"Jim Hamilton is one of the most faithful scholars of Scripture and expositors of God's Word. In this new work, he offers remarkable insight into the structure of the Gospel of John, implications for biblical theology, and encouragement for biblical exposition. Jim is committed to Scripture and to the marvelous display of the glory of God in biblical theology. This book will greatly encourage all who love and teach and preach the Gospel of John."

R. Albert Mohler Jr., president, The Southern Baptist Theological Seminary

"Jim Hamilton makes me love the Bible. That's because his joy for Scripture is infectious. It's also because he understands that the biblical authors didn't simply write truth; they wrote truth in a beautiful way. Their poetry and parallelism, creedal affirmations and chiasms were all employed in the service of exalting the glory of the Son of God made flesh. Jim's ruthlessly textual commitment to biblical theology, his steel-trap memory, and his literary sensibilities are a unique combination that gives rise to biblical and beautiful observations from the Gospel of John."

Sam Emadi, senior pastor, Hunsinger Lane Baptist Church

"Fascinating. Novel. Provocative. *In the Beginning Was the Word* is potentially a watershed publication on the literary structure of the Gospel of John. . . . Hamilton typifies scholarship that treasures the text and adores Jesus—the text's focus—and in this I hope readers follow his example."

S. D. Ellison, director of training, Irish Baptist College; author of *Raised According to the Scriptures*

"Jim Hamilton's book invites Christian scholars and novices alike to explore the wonder and beauty of John's Gospel, which is a river shallow enough for wading lambs yet deep enough for swimming elephants. After years of insightful study and with eyes trained to recognize how John, with words masterfully chosen and assembled, exquisitely portrays the One identified as 'the Word,' Hamilton contends that John crafted his entire Gospel as a large chiasm. . . . The extent of his structural analysis calls for mindful reflection, not a mere nod of the head or dismissive wave of the hand."

Ardel B. Caneday, University of Northwestern–St. Paul

"*In the Beginning Was the Word* is a unique and fresh contribution to biblical and pastoral studies, one which rewards a close reading. In the book, James Hamilton attempts to elucidate the layered but rich complexity of the theology of the Gospel of John through its literary form. . . . Hamilton's book should get wide appeal and hopefully regular use. I'm happy to recommend it and look forward to using it in the classroom and the pulpit."

Josh Philpot, pastor, Founders Baptist Church, Houston, Texas

IN THE BEGINNING WAS THE WORD

FINDING MEANING IN THE LITERARY STRUCTURE OF THE GOSPEL OF JOHN

JAMES M. HAMILTON JR.

Published by Baker Books
a division of Baker Publishing Group
Grand Rapids, Michigan
BakerBooks.com

Printed in the United States of America

Library of Congress Cataloging-in-Publication Data
Names: Hamilton, James M., 1974– author.
Title: In the beginning was the Word : finding meaning in the literary structure of the Gospel of John / James M. Hamilton Jr.
Description: Grand Rapids, Michigan : Baker Books, a division of Baker Publishing Group, [2025] | Includes bibliographical references.
Identifiers: LCCN 2024038998 | ISBN 9781540904867 (paperback) | ISBN 9781540905000 | ISBN 9781493450473 (ebook)
Subjects: LCSH: Bible. John—Theology. | Bible. John—Language, style. | Bible. John—Criticism, interpretation, etc. | Jesus Christ—Person and offices—Biblical teaching.
Classification: LCC BS2615.52 .H352 2025 | DDC 226.5/066—dc23/eng/20250215
LC record available at https://lccn.loc.gov/2024038998

Unless otherwise indicated, all Scripture translations are the author's own.

Cover design by Kathleen Lynch

Baker Publishing Group publications use paper produced from sustainable forestry practices and postconsumer waste whenever possible.

25 26 27 28 29 30 31 7 6 5 4 3 2 1

For
Mike and Mindy,
Levi, Emma, Hudson,
and Hannah

CONTENTS

I shall cry out the meaning of this day:
the fleshless one is made flesh,
the Word becomes material,
the invisible is seen,
the intangible is touched,
the timeless has a beginning,
the Son of God becomes Son of Man—
"Jesus Christ, yesterday and today, the same
also for all ages!"

—Gregory of Nazianzus (*Oration* 38.2)[1]

1. Quoted in R. B. Jamieson, *The Paradox of Sonship: Christology in the Epistle to the Hebrews*, Studies in Christian Doctrine and Scripture (Downers Grove, IL: InterVarsity, 2021), 40. Jamieson cites Brian E. Daley, *Gregory of Nazianzus*, The Early Church Fathers (London: Rutledge, 2006), 118.

1

AN INTRODUCTION TO JOHN'S THEOLOGY

> There is thus no inconsistence between creation and salvation; for the One Father has employed the same Agent for both works, effecting the salvation of the world through the same Word Who made it in the beginning.
>
> —Athanasius, *On the Incarnation* §1[1]

Here at the outset let us appreciate the audacity of the son of Zebedee called John, whose authorship of the Fourth Gospel I will treat as a given. Consider the boldness of this man. The closing words of his account of Jesus assert that were everything written, not even the world could contain the books (John 21:25). And his opening words declare of the one of whom he undertakes to write, "Through him all things were made" (1:3). The book narrates the salvation of the world by the most important person who has ever lived. And John attempted

1. Athanasius, *On the Incarnation: De Incarnatione Verbi Dei* (Crestwood, NY: St. Vladimir's Seminary Press, 1998), 26.

it. This magnificent achievement was inspired by the Holy Spirit and put to words by the beloved disciple. Glory be to the Father and to the Son and to the Holy Spirit: as it was in the beginning, is now, and ever shall be; world without end. Amen.

So let us appreciate the daring, the willingness to try, the effort expended to put into words the most significant series of events accomplished in any lifetime. The intrepid endeavor should not go unnoticed, to say nothing of the élan with which it has been carried off. If "true wit is nature to advantage dress'd, / What oft was thought, but ne'er so well express'd,"[2] John has shown it best. This Gospel tells the most important story in the most profound way.

As John thought about the task of communicating the significance of Jesus, to what precursors would he have looked? He may well have had access to the other canonical Gospels, but he no doubt had what we now refer to as the Old Testament. From Moses, the Prophets, and the Sages John came to appreciate the possibilities and power of the chiastic structure, and from the fertile fields of the broad, sunlit uplands in the Scriptures his mind was no doubt stocked with terminology and imagery, metaphor and pattern.

One day I hope to offer to John my congratulations and appreciation. I fully expect him to direct all praise to God in Christ through the Spirit, as he should, but I hope he also feels encouraged that we appreciated the difficulty of what he undertook, the profundity with which he accomplished it, and the elegance and

> The word "chiasm" derives from the Greek letter *chi*, which looks like an x. The idea is that the first and last points match, as do the second and second to last, with as many in between as the author desires, hinging at a central turning point. For more, simply keep reading.

2. Alexander Pope, "An Essay on Criticism (1711)," Poetry Foundation, published October 13, 2009, https://www.poetryfoundation.org/articles/69379/an-essay-on-criticism.

beauty that by God's grace he gave the world. What a book. And it goes without saying but must be said: As good as the Gospel of John is, the master whose story it tells is even better.

John has produced a book that brings together the world-historical import of a Genesis with the reflective depths of an Ecclesiastes. His is a book that radiates as much glory as the Psalter even as it scales theological heights with ease comparable to Isaiah, with the urgent passion and love of Deuteronomy joined to the symbolic power of Hosea. John was a man who meditated on the Scriptures, and in his beautiful book we read the words of someone shaped by them, a man who knew what it was to be loved by their fulfillment, a man who followed in the footsteps of his master and made God known to men.

There are four canonical Gospels that tell the story of Jesus, but the Gospel of John is without parallel. I take nothing away from the others or the achievement of their authors when I say that no other Gospel writer shows the daring of the son of Zebedee. Nothing in all the world's literature compares, for instance, to what we find in John 5:19–30, where John presents Jesus explaining that the Son joins the work the Father does because "the Father loves the Son and shows him all that he himself is doing" (5:20 ESV). Nowhere else in the world do readers find the Second Person of the Godhead saying of the First, "For as the Father has life in himself, so he has granted the Son also to have life in himself" (5:26 ESV). The words that John records Jesus saying in these and similar passages give unparalleled insight into the relations between Father, Son, and Holy Spirit, and it took some dash to do it.

So as we begin our consideration of the Gospel according to John, dear reader, let me encourage you to thank God for its author. Exert the imaginative effort to consider what it cost John to write this book: the life of preparation in the Scriptures and the expenditure of his experience of Jesus, from the exhilaration in the realization that the Messiah had come, to the agony of seeing him crucified, and then the wonder of the resurrection, and on to the massive burden of the responsibility to tell the story. Like his master, this man gave himself to us.

Biblical Theology

I am convinced that the task of biblical theology is the attempt to understand and embrace the interpretive perspective of the biblical authors.[3] This task involves understanding the master story the biblical authors assume and into which they plug their narratives, the truths and symbols that derive from that story, the ethical behaviors and acts of worship that correspond to it, and the culture it produces.

Literary Structure and Fulfillment of the Old Testament

For a biblical theology of the Gospel of John, we will need to establish the literary structure of the Gospel, because the arrangement of the material is a major factor in what the author communicates. We need to understand both *what* John communicates and *how* he communicates it. This book will argue that understanding the literary contours of John's Gospel will put us in position to understand the way that he engages with, and claims to present fulfillment of, earlier Scripture. John's interpretation of Scripture pervades his presentation, and he typically engages earlier passages in ways that are as artistic as they are surprising, as revelatory as they are insightful, and as simple as they are profound. It starts with his re-presentation of Genesis 1:1–3 in John 1:1–5, where John's "in the beginning" evokes that same phrase at the beginning of the Bible.

> Biblical theology is the attempt to understand and embrace the interpretive perspective of the biblical authors.

3. See further James M. Hamilton Jr., *What Is Biblical Theology?* (Wheaton: Crossway, 2014).

A Preview of This Project

This project, like John's Gospel, is a chiasm. The first two chapters introduce the body of the study, the final two respond to it. After this first introductory chapter, the second will preview the chiastic structure of John's Gospel before considering its central turning point. The component parts of that wide-angle chiasm are themselves chiastically structured, and chapters 3–8 will work through these. The body of the study, therefore, examines how the literary structure of John's Gospel conveys John's theology. The final two chapters respond to the theology of John's Gospel by reflecting on the incarnation in chapter 9 and the Trinity in chapter 10.

Presenting this book's chiastic structure will provide an overview of its contents:

Chapter 1, An Introduction to John's Theology
- Chapter 2, The Literary Structure of the Gospel of John
  - Chapter 3, Grace upon Grace: The Word Tabernacling and Spirit Filled in John 1
    - Chapter 4, From Cana to Cana: Beholding and Believing in John 2–4
      - Chapter 5, Life from the Dead: In Public, Among Crowds, at Feasts in John 5–11
      - Chapter 6, The Hour Has Come: In Private, with Disciples, at Passover in John 12–17
    - Chapter 7, From Garden to Garden: Jesus Arrested, Crucified, and Raised in John 18:1–20:18
  - Chapter 8, The Temple of the Holy Spirit: Jesus Sends as He Was Sent in John 20:19–21:25
- Chapter 9, The Word Became Flesh: The Incarnation in the Gospel of John

Chapter 10, The Trinity in John's Gospel

The chiastic structure of chapters 3–8 of this book derives from the content of John's Gospel, and the material in these chapters matches the literary structure of the Gospel itself. Chapters 1 and 10 correspond to each other in that what is introduced in chapter 1 culminates in the knowledge of the Triune God in chapter 10. Chapter 2, which overviews the literary structure of John's Gospel, matches chapter 9, which considers the incarnation, because in the same way that John's Gospel took the form of a chiasm when John's ideas became a book, so the Second Person of the Godhead took the form of a man when the Word became flesh.

Discipleship in John's Gospel

John wrote in obedience to what Jesus commands his disciples to do in Matthew 28:18–20, that people might believe, and believing have life (John 20:31). As I have noted, the body of this book will work through the Gospel of John according to its own literary structure, then the final two chapters will consider the incarnation and the Trinity. Though this section comes in the first chapter, it was the last to be written. Having completed the project, in this section I will suggest an image that informs how this study can be applied in the life of faith. The hope is that readers will be alerted to the ramifications of the study here at the beginning so that they can ruminate on them as they make their way through the book, and may meditative consideration thereby deepen impact.

Jesus came in fulfillment of the ministry of the temple (John 2:19–21) and its priests (e.g., 17:1–26). As with the temple, the Spirit came down upon Jesus to abide on him (1:32–33), and Jesus fulfilled the sacrifices for sin that make atonement (1:29). Jesus then sent his disciples as he was sent (20:21), imparted to them the indwelling Spirit (20:22), and granted them authority to forgive and retain sin (20:23). The temple was a place where God dwelled among his people, where he was known, where reconciliation between God and man was sought and found. This ministry Jesus fulfilled and passed on to his disciples. And thus John's friend, Peter, told those to whom he wrote that they were being made into both a temple and a priesthood: "You yourselves like living stones are being built up as a spiritual house, to be a holy priesthood, to offer spiritual sacrifices acceptable to God through Jesus Christ" (1 Pet. 2:5 ESV).

To help his audience understand these realities, John depicts a relationship of loving communion between the Father, Jesus, and the Spirit, and this experience of being "one" the Father through Christ by the Spirit extends to the disciples (John 17:11, 21–23). In John 1:18, Jesus is described as "the only begotten God in the bosom of the Father" who has "made him known." John makes it clear that those who receive Jesus are born again (1:12–13; 3:3–8), and in 1 John 5:18 he speaks of them as "begotten," with language similar to the way Jesus was "begotten." Jesus and those who receive him are not begotten of God in all the same ways, but both are born of God. The beloved disciple who testifies in John's Gospel is making Jesus known through what he writes (20:30–31; 21:24), and this beloved disciple describes himself "reclining in the bosom of Jesus" (13:23) in the same terms used to speak of Jesus "in the bosom of the Father" (1:18). This suggests that to abide in Christ (cf. 8:31; 15:7) is to relate to Jesus the way that he relates to his Father, and the beloved disciple is modestly put forward as an example for the Gospel's audience to follow. The temple imagery also helps with the concept of abiding: If Jesus comes as the fulfillment of the temple, then to abide in him is to live out Psalm 84:4, "Blessed are those who dwell in your house, ever singing your praise!" (ESV).

Jesus fulfills the ministry of the temple by fulfilling its sacrificial system to take away the sins of the world (John 1:29). The disciples do not give their lives as any kind of sacrifice for sin, but Jesus does call them to follow him in the fruit bearing of dying to rise on behalf of others. When he announces that the time has come for the Son of Man to be glorified in John 12:23, he goes on to speak of himself metaphorically as a grain of wheat that must fall into the ground and die to bear fruit in 12:24. He then applies this message to his followers in 12:25–26: "Whoever loves his life loses it, and whoever hates his life in this world will keep it for eternal life. If anyone serves me, he must follow me; and where I am, there will my servant be also. If anyone serves me, the Father will honor him" (ESV). The Father is about to glorify Jesus through the self-giving death through which he will bear much fruit (cf. 12:28–33). Jesus tells his disciples that this pattern of self-giving is to be their way of life as well, not to take away sins but to love others as he has loved them. And Jesus promises that this will enable them to be where he is and, with him, be honored by the Father (12:26). The self-giving love displays the glory of God and creates the unity, for both of which Jesus prays in John 17.

Jesus washes his disciples' feet and tells them they are to do likewise for one another (13:14), not that they might literally wash one another's feet but that they might serve one another as he has served them (13:15–17). Jesus shows his disciples the love than which there is none greater, laying down his life for his friends (15:13), and he prefaces that explanation with the directive that his disciples are to love one another as he has loved them (15:12).

Jesus tells Pilate that his purpose in coming into the world is to bear witness to the truth (18:37). The beloved disciple repeatedly asserts that he is bearing witness to the truth (19:35; 21:24). Jesus was sent by the Father to bear witness to the truth (10:36), and Jesus sent the beloved disciple (and the others) as he himself was sent (20:21).

Jesus sent his disciples as he was sent, that they might live as he lived, serve as he served, speak as he spoke, and die as he died, so that people might have the eternal life of knowing God in Christ (17:3). Christlike self-giving will enable the disciples to be one as Jesus and the Father are one (17:21), and the glory that the Father gave to Jesus when Jesus gave himself for the world

(13:31–32) is the glory Jesus will give to his disciples when they do the same (17:22). The opportunity to show the greatest love, to be obedient even unto death, to love as Christ loves, this is the glory of Christ that he gives to his disciples (17:22), whereby they are in him, and whereby they are one with each other and attested by God (17:23).

The Spirit gives life that all this might happen (6:63): sent from the Father (15:26) in the name of Jesus (14:26) as the Spirit of truth (14:17) to bear witness to the truth (15:26) and lead the disciples into all truth (14:26; 16:7, 13) to glorify Jesus (16:14).

When the disciples receive the indwelling Spirit (14:17; 20:22), Jesus and the Father will make their home in them (14:23), making them the temple, the dwelling place of God on earth, where forgiveness of sins can be found (20:23). Jesus came as the fulfillment of the temple and its ministry, and he sent his followers as he was sent, imparting to them the indwelling Spirit and granting them authority to forgive sin. As believers in Jesus meditate on the sanctifying Word of God (17:17), Christ abides in them, and they in him (8:31; 15:7).

Questions for Reflection and Discussion

1. Have you ever considered memorizing whole chapters of the Gospel of John, or even the whole book? If you've studied Greek, have you thought about memorizing it in Greek?
2. Which gets more of your time: reading, studying, memorizing, and meditating on the Bible, or reading things written about the Bible and listening to what other people say about the Bible? Which of those two things is true of the blessed man in Psalm 1?
3. Have you thought about how John went about writing his Gospel? How do you imagine him undertaking this task?

Suggested Reading

Hamilton, James M., Jr. *God's Glory in Salvation through Judgment: A Biblical Theology*. Wheaton: Crossway, 2010.

Hamilton, James M., Jr. *God's Indwelling Presence: The Holy Spirit in the Old and New Testaments*. NAC Studies in Bible and Theology. Nashville: B&H, 2006.

Hamilton, James M., Jr. *Typology—Understanding the Bible's Promise-Shaped Patterns: How Old Testament Expectations Are Fulfilled in Christ*. Grand Rapids: Zondervan, 2022.

Hamilton, James M., Jr. *What Is Biblical Theology?* Wheaton: Crossway, 2014.

2

THE LITERARY STRUCTURE OF THE GOSPEL OF JOHN

> What is important is that the Fathers followed the meaning of Scripture, beginning with the evidence which I have just extracted from the Scriptures and presented to you.
>
> —Basil of Caesarea, *On the Holy Spirit*[1]

We cannot understand John's theology without an understanding of the literary structure of his Gospel, because the literary structure of the Gospel is not merely the transport vehicle delivering the freight of the theology; it is an essential part of the message itself. To rightly understand *what* John has communicated, we must understand *how* he has communicated it. To read English poetry we must know the English language and English poetic forms. To read biblical literature we must know the biblical languages and the literary forms employed by the biblical authors. The possibilities and limitations of language and form provide parameters for what authors can

1. Basil of Caesarea, *On the Holy Spirit*, trans. David Anderson (Crestwood, NY: St. Vladimir's Seminary Press, 1980), 34.

do with their messages, and when working with known forms, authors intend their audiences to interpret in accordance with how the medium creates a kind of biosphere in which the message lives and moves and has its being.

The Gospel according to John evidences intentional, strategic, purposeful arrangement, from the first word to the last, and the whole thing is one wide-angle chiasm made up of smaller units that are themselves chiasms built of chiasms. In this chapter I will first briefly explore what chiasms are and how they function. From there I will discuss how we as interpreters establish that an author has intended to structure his material this way, before offering my proposal for the chiastic structure of the whole Gospel, which chapters 3–8 of this book will exposit and defend. This chapter will conclude by examining the central unit of the chiastic structure of John's Gospel (John 11:45–12:19).

What Chiasms Are and Why Authors Use Them

The word "chiasm" derives from the name of the Greek letter *chi*, which is shaped like an *x*: χ. The chiastic form refers to a progression of statements that can be plotted along the left side of that *chi*-shaped letter, with the first statement or word matching the last, the second matching the second to last, and so on, for as many intervals as there may be to a centerpoint, which is often the most important idea or the one on which everything turns. These central statements typically allude back to the beginning and forward to the end.

Chiasms are extensions of parallelism that provide structure and boundaries within which authors work and, when recognized, can function as mnemonic aids to an audience, enabling authors to create both synergy between corresponding parts and an artistically beautiful, intellectually satisfying finished product. This statement can be exposited by putting it into chiastic shape.

Chiasms are:

Extensions of parallelism
    Providers of structure and boundaries
        Aids to memory
    Creators of synergy
Vehicles for artistic beauty

If as the author it was my intention for these descriptors to appear in a certain order because I had a chiastic structure in mind (and it was), then it was also part of my intention to suggest that the first and last are to be read together, as are the second and second to last. With minimal effort, one could use this structure to establish its statements in memory, accomplishing its centerpoint. Parallelism is a literary form that juxtaposes related statements and adorns writing with artistic beauty, and extending parallelism increases that beauty. Similarly, structure and boundaries provide context within which synergy happens. And if I want my audience to remember the structure of my statements, giving them an architecture that facilitates memory is a good practice. The intellectual satisfaction of the concluding statement forming a latch with the opening creates the impression of completeness. Everything that needed to be said has been said, even if there was more that could have been said.

For a biblical author with as much to say as John (cf. John 21:25), such a structure is vital. I have been studying the Gospel of John for decades now, and in the process of grasping its chiastic structures, I have a new and firmer mental hold on the Gospel's contents, so that I can easily reproduce them simply by taking a mental stroll through the components of the structure in relationship to one another.[2]

2. See further the discussion of a "memory palace" in Joshua Foer, *Moonwalking with Einstein: The Art and Science of Remembering Everything* (New York: Penguin, 2011).

Establishing Authorial Intent in Chiastic Structures

Whereas authors today give order and shape to their content by providing chapter titles, subheadings, and paragraphing formats (indented first lines, blank spaces between paragraphs, etc.), some of which are enumerated in relationship to one another, the biblical authors built their content with repeated terms, phrases, or concepts that were intended to enable audiences to establish where one unit began and ended.[3] Within that unit, similar use of strategic repetition would enable authors to mark their progress through each successive episode or concept. For examples of what I am talking about in this section, I refer readers to the next two sections of this chapter, and then to the content of chapters 3–8.

As we study these texts, we want to determine the parameters of the units of thought and then consider those units in relationship to one another. The first step is to attempt to establish boundaries

PROCEDURE FOR DISCOVERING LITERARY STRUCTURE

1. Determine the boundaries of the units of thought.
2. Examine those units for verbal repetitions that might point to the microstructure of the unit.
3. Consider the units in relationship to one another to discern micro- and macrostructure.
4. Look for repetitions of words, phrases, and concepts—both synonymous and antonymous—and see if they appear in corresponding sections of material.

3. My view is that Moses employed these literary strategies and techniques and that the biblical authors who followed him and perpetuated the worldview he taught learned them from him. See further the first and last chapters, on micro- and macro-level indicators for establishing authorial intent, in James M. Hamilton Jr., *Typology—Understanding the Bible's Promise-Shaped Patterns: How Old Testament Expectations Are Fulfilled in Christ* (Grand Rapids: Zondervan, 2022), 1–32, 331–60.

by finding beginning and ending statements, and often these will be repeated words, exact phrases, or at least similar concepts. Once we think we have found the end of a unit, if that is followed by a new point of departure, such as a change in topic, or some other indicator that the author is moving in a new direction, we can proceed on the working hypothesis that we have found a unit of thought. We can then examine that unit to see if, within it, there are repetitions or recurring words, phrases, or concepts that structure what the author communicates.

Recognizing repetitions requires us to retain in our minds the phrases, constructions, and concepts we have already read, and the more retention that happens the better. I have found it useful to copy and paste the biblical text and then mark repeated words, phrases, and concepts with different colored fonts and highlights on the screen. This helps me to see the repetitions in relationship to one another. In my work on John's Gospel, I did this for the entirety of the Greek text of John, working up from the smaller to the larger units of thought: establishing boundaries, examining repetitions, trying to find the intrinsic indicators of how John intended his material to be grouped, how he intended his audience to associate units with one another. This kind of extremely rewarding close examination, one worth doing for its own sake, is foundational to understanding what John intended to communicate. It also facilitates reflection that enables deeper understanding of his theology.

The paragraphs, verse and chapter numbers, and subtitles that we find in English translations of the Bible were put there not by the biblical authors but by later, uninspired editors and translators. The verse and chapter divisions are often helpful but do not always correspond to units intended by the biblical authors. Sometimes the inserted subheadings, chapter breaks, and verse numbers break up the biblical author's natural flow of thought.

In the next section I propose a chiastic structure for the Gospel of John. This structure indicates that John balanced beginning, middle, and end, with a central turning point. The parallelism has its own inherent, artistic beauty, worthy of the glory of the one whose story it tells.

The Chiastic Structure of John's Gospel

Before presenting the chiastic structure of the Gospel, allow me to briefly summarize pertinent aspects of its corresponding elements, beginning with first and last, moving through the intervening sections to its central unit, which will be discussed in the next section.

In John 1, Jesus is the Word become flesh who tabernacles among us (1:1, 14), on whom the Spirit comes down to remain (1:32–33). In the corresponding final unit of John's Gospel, Jesus breathes on his disciples and tells them to receive the Holy Spirit (20:22), sending them as the Father sent him (20:21), authorizing them to forgive sin (20:23). Jesus is a human fulfillment of the temple, sent by the Father and indwelled by the Spirit at the beginning, and his disciples are likewise at the end.

The second unit of John's Gospel, John 2–4, corresponds to the second to last, John 18:1–20:18. John 2–4 begins and ends in Cana with signs that are enumerated first (2:11) and second (4:54). John 18:1–20:18 begins and ends in a garden, and in both the first and last garden scenes of this unit, Jesus asks someone whom they are seeking: Judas in 18:4, Mary in 20:15. Most significantly, after cleansing the temple, Jesus speaks of the temple of his body when he says in 2:19, "Destroy this temple, and in three days I will raise it up" (ESV; cf. 2:17–21). This is exactly what happens in 18:1–20:18, and in both 2:22 and 20:9 John notes that the disciples understood the relevant Scripture only after Jesus was raised from the dead.

The third and third-to-last sections comprise two balancing large middle sections that run from chapters 5 to 11 and 12 to 17, each notably bracketed as large units of related text. Once those brackets have been identified, the distinctive contrasting features of the two corresponding sections come into focus. First the brackets, then the contrasting features. In John 5, having healed the man at the Pool of Bethesda, Jesus asserts in 5:25, "An hour is coming, and is now here, when the dead will hear the voice of the Son of God, and those who hear will live" (ESV). That very thing happens when Jesus calls Lazarus from the tomb in 11:43–44. Matching the "resurrection" brackets around John 5–11 are the "hour has come" brackets around John 12–17. In John 12, once the Greeks have come seeking Jesus, he declares in 12:23, "The hour has come for the Son of Man to be glorified" (ESV). This statement is slightly rephrased in John 17:1 when Jesus prays, "Father, the hour has come; glorify your Son that the Son may glorify you" (ESV). With these statements bookending John 5–11 and 12–17, we can then compare and contrast those chapters with one another, and we see that in John 5–11 Jesus is in public, among crowds, at a number of different feasts. In John 12–17, by contrast, Jesus is in private, with his disciples, at the final Passover.

This leaves the section of John 11:45–12:19 at the center of the Gospel. There are four units here, the first and last matching each other, the middle two standing together. In the first, Caiaphas prophesies that it is better that one man die than that the whole nation perish (11:50). This is matched by Jesus enacting the fulfillment of Zechariah 9:9 at the triumphal entry (John 12:15). At the center of the Gospel we see John showing his audience what he told them in 1:10–13 (which, incidentally, is the center of the chiastic structure of the introductory unit of 1:1–18): Jesus came to his own, and his own received him not (1:10–11), but to those who received him, he gave the right to become children of God (1:12–13). Thus the telling, and in the showing John relates how some were seeking to kill Jesus in 11:53–57. They received him not. Those who received him, by contrast, are represented by Martha, Mary, and Lazarus, who gave a dinner for him, at which Mary anointed him for burial, in 12:1–8.

The chiastic structure of John's Gospel can be depicted as follows:

John 1, The Word tabernacling and Spirit filled
John 2–4, From Cana to Cana; destroy this temple, and I will raise it in three days
John 5–11, In public; among crowds; at feasts
John 11:45–53, Better that one die
John 11:54–57, Passover; rejection
John 12:1–8, Anointing; reception
John 12:9–19, Triumphal entry
John 12–17, In private; with disciples; at Passover
John 18–20, From garden to garden; temple destroyed and raised on third day
John 20–21, The temple of the Holy Spirit; Jesus sends as he was sent

We will consider John 5–11 at length in chapter 5, but here I offer a preview of the way these chapters form a chiasm unto themselves.

5:1–47, The dead will hear the voice of the Son of God and live
6:1–71, I am the bread of life
7:1–52, If anyone is thirsty, let him come to me and drink
8:12–59, I am the light of the world
9:1–41, Sight for the man born blind
10:1–42, I am the good shepherd
11:1–44, Lazarus, come forth

Similarly, John 12–17 will be discussed in chapter 6, but here follows an anticipatory glance at the chiasm these chapters compose.

12:20–50, The hour has come for the Son of Man to be glorified

13:1–38, Footwashing; Jesus prepares his disciples

14:1–31, Let not your hearts be troubled

15:1–15, I am the true vine

15:16–27, If the world hates you

16:1–33, Jesus prepares his disciples for his death and resurrection

17:1–26, The hour has come; glorify your Son that your Son may glorify you

One fascinating thing to observe about these two structures is that at the center of both John places the importance of abiding in Christ by means of his word. In John 8:31 Jesus says, "If you abide in my word, you are truly my disciples" (ESV). Then in John 15:1–15 he teaches his disciples that he is the vine, that they are the branches, and that they must abide in him by ensuring that his words abide in them (cf. esp. 15:7).

In addition to being chiasms unto themselves, John 5–11 and 12–17 also join together to form a wide-angle chiasm that is depicted in table 2.1 on the next page (for discussion, see the concluding section of chap. 6).

The Center of John's Chiasm at 11:45–12:19

As we turn our attention to the central section of John's Gospel, the units of thought in relationship to one another should be borne in mind:

The Center of the Gospel of John

11:45–53, Better that one die

11:54–57, Passover; rejection

12:1–8, Anointing; reception

12:9–19, Triumphal entry

Table 2.1: John 5–11 and 12–17

A	5:1–47, As the Father has life in himself, so he granted the Son to have life in himself
B	6:1–71, I am the bread of life
C	7:1–52, If anyone is thirsty, let him come to me and drink
D	8:12–59, I am the light of the world
C′	9:1–41, Sight for the man born blind
B′	10:1–42, The good shepherd
A′	11:1–44, Raising of Lazarus
	11:45–53, Better that one die
	11:54–57, Passover
	12:1–8, Anointing
	12:9–19, Triumphal entry
a	12:20–50, A grain of wheat
b	13:1–38, Footwashing
c	14:1–31, Let not your hearts be troubled
d′	15:1–15, I am the true vine
c′	15:16–27, If the world hates you
b′	16:1–33, Jesus prepares his disciples for his death and resurrection
a′	17:1–26, The hour has come; glorify your Son that your Son may glorify you

Consideration of each of these units will deepen our ability to understand John's message. In modern Johannine scholarship there has been much discussion of the raising of Lazarus as the catalyst of the crucifixion in the Gospel of John. That wider discussion reflects the impact of John's literary structure, where immediately following the raising of Lazarus, John presents a conversation between the opponents of Jesus that involves the Pharisees, the chief priests, and the high priest himself in John 11:45–53. At the beginning of this conversation the parties are asking one another what they should do about Jesus (11:45–47), and at its end they have resolved to have him executed (11:53). After asking what they should do, their second statement communicates their concern that all will be convinced by Jesus, prompting the Romans to take away the Jewish place and nation (11:48). In the matching statement in the chiasm's second-to-last position, John observes in 11:52 that Jesus' death will be not only for Jews but for all the scattered children of God, that they might be gathered as one. The third and third-to-last statements in 11:49 and 11:51, which frame the central line at 11:50, contain no little irony. In 11:49, Caiaphas the high priest tells his dialogue partners, "You know nothing at all!" Then in 11:51, John remarks that Caiaphas did not speak the words of 11:50 "from himself," which points out that Caiaphas did not himself know what was happening. John thus centers the prophecy of Caiaphas in 11:50, where he asserts that it would be better for Jesus to die for the people than for the whole nation to perish. The chiastic structure of John 11:45–53 can be summarized as follows:

11:45–53, Better That One Die

11:45–47, What shall we do?
  11:48, All will believe in him
    11:49, You know nothing at all
      11:50, Better that one die than that the whole nation perish
    11:51, He spoke not of himself
  11:52, Not for the Jews only but for all God's children
11:53, They made plans to put him to death

The seeds of the resolve to kill Jesus, which had been sown and begun to sprout (see 5:18; 7:1, 25; 8:37, 40, 59; 10:31), now flower into the determination articulated in 11:53.

In 11:54–57 John narrates again the way that Jesus avoids conflict until the time has come. The first and last statements of this unit relate how Jesus no longer walks openly among the Jews (11:54a) because the order has gone out that his whereabouts are to be reported that he might be seized (11:57). Thus, Jesus retreats to the wilderness to abide with his disciples (11:54b) while his opponents are seeking him (11:56). This arrangement places John's remark in 11:55 in central position: "Now the Passover of the Jews was near, and many went up to Jerusalem from the country before the Passover that they might sanctify themselves." Note that "Passover" appears twice in this verse, and the purpose statement that the people went to sanctify themselves portends what will be accomplished. The chiastic structure of John 11:54–57 can be depicted as follows:

11:54–57, Passover at Hand

11:54a, No longer openly among Jews
  11:54b, Abided with disciples
    11:55, Passover at hand
  11:56, They were seeking him
11:57, That they might seize him

I note above that the rejection and reception of Jesus in John 1:10–13 is the centerpoint of the chiastic structure of John 1:1–18. That initial centerpoint prepares John's audience for the centerpoint of the whole Gospel, where Jesus' Jewish opponents, having rejected him and resolved to kill him in 11:45–53, look to seize him at the Passover in 11:54–57. In the corresponding units, those who have received him celebrate him and anoint him for burial in 12:1–8, and then he enters the city in triumph, ironically, like a lamb that is led to slaughter, in 12:9–19.

John 12:1–8 is an amazing piece of narrative. Standing across from the mentions of Passover and of Lazarus, whom Jesus raised from the dead in 12:1, is the reference to the burial of Jesus in 12:7–8, provoking all kinds of reflections: How can the one who raised the dead die? If Jesus raised Lazarus, will he not himself be raised? How long can death hope to hold him? What is the significance of his death and burial?

In second and second-to-last positions in this structure we find a studied contrast between those giving a dinner for Jesus, the likes of Martha and Lazarus in John 12:2, and the explanation in 12:6 that Judas was not concerned for the poor but was a thief who used to steal from the moneybag he stewarded. Martha and Lazarus serve Jesus and show hospitality to him, while Judas steals from him.

These contrasts are extended into the third and third-to-last statements, with Mary anointing Jesus in 12:3a and Judas complaining about the waste in 12:4–5. John establishes more about character, motivations, and priorities by means of this "showing" than he ever could by "telling."

The central statement in this chiastic structure hearkens back to the way that Jesus has been presented as the fulfillment of the temple (see esp. the discussion of John 1 in chap. 3 below). Not only is Jesus the temple who will be torn down and raised on the third day (2:17–22; 18:1–20:18), when this happens the significance and meaning of the Day of Atonement will be fulfilled. In the instructions for the Day of Atonement in Leviticus 16, Aaron was to offer a bull as a sin offering for himself (Lev. 16:6), and then two goats were selected (16:7–10). Having made atonement for himself by killing the bull as a sin offering (16:11), we read in Leviticus 16:12–13, "And he shall take a censer full of coals of fire from the altar before the Lord, and two handfuls of sweet incense beaten small, and he shall bring it inside the veil and put the incense on the fire before the Lord, that the cloud of the incense may cover the mercy seat that is over the testimony, so that he does not die" (ESV). This filling of the temple with the cloud of incense seems to be alluded to when John notes that as Mary anointed the feet of Jesus, "the house was filled with the aroma of the ointment" (John 12:3b). As with a number of symbolic statements in John, we are dealing not with the literal thing but with a symbol that points to it. In this case, the house is not literally the temple, but its filling with fragrance points to the real thing signified.

The chiasm in John 12:1–8 is as follows:

12:1–8, Mary Anoints Jesus at Bethany

12:1, Lazarus raised

  12:2, Dinner given

    12:3a, Mary anointed Jesus

      12:3b, Fragrance filled the house

    12:4–5, Judas complained

  12:6, Judas stole

12:7–8, Jesus' burial

And so we come to the triumphal entry. The lamb before its shearers will be silent, like a sheep to slaughter, but no one takes his life from him. He lays it down of his own accord (10:18). John centers this idea by placing the fulfillment of key scriptural texts at the center of the chiastic structure in 12:9–19. As the people enact the fulfillment of Psalm 118:25–26 in John 12:13, Jesus initiates the fulfillment of Zechariah 9:9 in John 12:14–15. Framing the fulfillments, the crowd gathers to celebrate Jesus in John 12:12, and after the "entry texts" are enacted, the disciples remember these things after Jesus is glorified in 12:16. The account opens and closes, in 12:9–11 and 12:17–19, the same way: with mention of the crowd, of Lazarus who was raised from the dead, of the chief priests and Pharisees, and of how "many" are believing in Jesus and "the world" has gone after him (matching the concerns articulated in the corresponding section at 11:45, 48). The chiastic structure of John 12:9–19 can be depicted as follows:

12:9–19, The Triumphal Entry

12:9–11, The crowd; Lazarus raised; chief priests; many believed in Jesus

  12:12, The crowd acts to fulfill Scripture

    12:13, Hosanna; Psalm 118:25–26

12:14–15, Jesus enacts Zechariah 9:9

12:16, When Jesus was glorified, the disciples remembered

12:17–19, The crowd; Lazarus raised; Pharisees; the world has gone after Jesus

Conclusion

John's Gospel is like a magnificent cathedral, everything beautifully proportioned, perfectly balanced, with flying buttresses and soaring arches, every beam in place, the architecture pointing beyond itself to the transcendent glory of the one it celebrates. As with a cathedral, the point is not to study the architecture by merely dissecting the construction. We must enter in and allow both the sobering elegance of lofty ceilings and the priceless grandeur of it all to do their work on us. We want to feel small in the vastness, to be moved by the resonance of the acoustics, to hear the echoes in the silences and the reverberations of the songs.

The art points beyond itself to the story it tells, and the story beyond itself again to the God it makes known. John invites us into his Gospel that we might know God (17:3), that the truth might set us free (8:32), that we might be sanctified by it (17:17), that we might be one in the glory of the Father and the Son (17:22–23). The only path is the way, the truth, and the life (14:6), that we might be where he is to see his glory (17:24), that we might dwell in the house of the Lord forever (14:2–3).

Questions for Reflection and Discussion

1. If this chapter was not your first exposure to chiastic structures, when did you first encounter them? Do you find

the idea that whole books can be structured as chiasms preposterous, plausible, likely, compelling, or obvious?

2. If an author has structured part of his book chiastically, how might he have structured the rest of it? Is it likely that an author would go to the trouble of structuring a whole section of a book chiastically but have a more or less haphazard arrangement for the rest?
3. Have you personally memorized a passage such as John 1:1–18 and then reflected on the relationships between the beginning and end and the intervening parts?

Suggested Reading

Berman, Joshua. "Criteria for Establishing Chiastic Structure: Lamentations 1 and 2 as Test Cases." *Maarav* 21 (2014): 57–69.

Blomberg, Craig. "The Structure of 1 Corinthians 1–7." *Criswell Theological Review* 4 (1989): 3–20.

Brouwer, Wayne. "Understanding Chiasm and Assessing Macro-Chiasm as a Tool of Biblical Interpretation." *Calvin Theological Journal* 53 (2018): 99–127.

Douglas, Mary. *Thinking in Circles: An Essay on Ring Composition.* New Haven: Yale University Press, 2010.

3

GRACE UPON GRACE

The Word Tabernacling and Spirit Filled in John 1

> The invisible one was made visible in the flesh;
> he who is from the heavens and from on high was in the
> likeness of earthly things;
> the immaterial one would be touched;
> he who is free in his own nature came in the form of a slave;
> he who blesses all creation became accursed;
> he who is all righteousness was numbered among transgressors;
> life itself came in the appearance of death.
>
> —Cyril of Alexandria, *On the Unity of Christ*[1]

In the first chapter of the Fourth Gospel, John's literary structure serves his presentation of Jesus as the one who brings fulfillment of all God promised in the Old Testament. Chiastic structures have been recognized for John 1:1–18, but to my knowledge the

1. Cyril of Alexandria, *On the Unity of Christ*, trans. John Anthony McGuckin (Crestwood, NY: St. Vladimir's Seminary Press, 1995), 61.

insight has not been applied to the whole of John 1, to say nothing of the rest of the Gospel, in anything like a thoroughgoing way.[2] The first step for determining literary structure is establishing the boundaries of literary units. Once we have established the boundaries of units, we can consider the units in relationship to one another.

Thinking of the opening chapters of John's Gospel, seeking to establish where the first major section ends, we observe that a new unit clearly opens at John 2:1. The time reference and the geographic location set the scene for the first sign at a wedding that takes place on the third day at Cana (2:1–12). The beginning of John 2 closely matches the end of John 4, where we find a second sign, again at Cana, and again on the third day (4:45–54). This indicates that John 1:1–51 could comprise the first unit, with John 2–4 the second.

If John 1:1–51 is the Gospel's first unit, are there subunits within it? The first 18 verses of John 1 have a continuity of theme unto themselves that focuses on Jesus as the Word. These verses introduce the Word who was with God (1:1) and became flesh (1:14), and this unit (1:1–18) introduces not only the first chapter but the whole of John's Gospel.[3] The topic of discussion shifts from the Word to the testimony of the Baptist at 1:19, and then the following three units of text are signaled by the phrase "the next day" at 1:29, 1:35, and 1:43. These textual markers denote five sections in John 1 (1–18, 19–28, 29–34, 35–42, 43–51), and understanding the chiastic structure of these five units of John 1 enables us to see

2. I made gestures in the direction of the Gospel being chiastically structured but had not yet found the key that unlocks the mystery in James M. Hamilton Jr., "John," in *John–Acts*, by James M. Hamilton Jr. and Brian J. Vickers, ESV Expository Commentary 9, ed. Iain M. Duguid, James M. Hamilton Jr., and Jay Sklar (Wheaton: Crossway, 2019), 19–308.

3. The chiastic structure of John 1:1–18 has been discussed by R. Alan Culpepper, "The Pivot of John's Prologue," *New Testament Studies* 27 (1980): 1–31; and Jeff Staley, "The Structure of John's Prologue: Its Implications for the Gospel's Narrative Structure," *Catholic Biblical Quarterly* 48 (1986): 241–64.

more clearly exactly what John intends to communicate about how Jesus comes in fulfillment of the Old Testament. Stated plainly to preview the argument, starting with the middle and working to the outer edges, the thesis of this chapter is that

> John employs a chiastic literary structure in the first chapter of his Gospel to present Jesus as the one on whom the Spirit has come down to remain (1:29–34), constituting him as God's true tabernacle (1:1–18), the fulfillment of precursors to the tabernacle such as Bethel (1:43–51), as the Baptist himself testifies (1:19–28, 35–42).

How does this relate to scriptural fulfillment? The Old Testament anticipates a new age of the Spirit when the Messiah comes (e.g., Isa. 11:1–2; 32:1, 15; Joel 2:28), and the narratives concerning the tabernacle in the book of Exodus create a close relationship between the priest and the dwelling place of God's Spirit, the tabernacle. The priest's clothing is made of the same material from which the tabernacle is constructed (cf. Exod. 26:1, 31; 28:5–6); the priest, like the tabernacle and its implements, is to be anointed with oil (28:41; 29:7; 30:22–33); and just as blood from the sacrifices of consecration is put on the horns of the altar, on its base, and on its sides (29:12, 16), so also blood is put on the tip of the priests' right ears, on the thumbs of their right hands, and on the big toes of their right feet (29:19–21). This close relationship between the Aaronic priesthood and the old covenant dwelling place of God informs the fulfillment of both the priesthood and the tabernacle in Christ, a theme that John heralds in the first literary unit of his account of the Word made flesh.

In the first chapter of his Gospel, John presents Jesus as the Word who has come to tabernacle (1:14), the fulfillment of the house of God (Bethel; cf. 1:51), on whom the Spirit has come down to remain (1:33). Not only is Jesus the fulfillment of the dwelling place of God (1:14), true priest and true temple, he is the expected

Prophet (1:21), the anticipated king Messiah (1:41), the Son of God (1:49), and the Lamb of God (1:29, 36).

We will see that the five units of John 1:1–51 are five individual chiasms that comprise one overarching chiasm. The overarching chiasm will be introduced here, and then will follow exposition of the five units—each of which is a chiasm unto itself—from which the one that encompasses the whole chapter is built.

The Chiastic Structure of John 1

As suggested in the previous section, the literary structure of John 1:1–51 may be depicted as follows:

> 1:1–18, The Word tabernacled in glory
>> 1:19–28, The voice crying in the wilderness
>>> 1:29–34, The descent of the Spirit to remain on Jesus
>>
>> 1:35–42, The Baptist's disciples follow Jesus
>
> 1:43–51, The true Bethel of whom Moses and the Prophets wrote

This literary structure centers the descent of the Spirit on Christ in 1:29–34, the unit that stands in the middle, framed on either side by the testimony of the Baptist, with beginning and ending units that deal with the dwelling place of God. The first and last units (1:1–18, 43–51) of this chiastic structure present Jesus coming in fulfillment of those places in the Old Testament where God was covenantally present with his people. The first unit concerns the way the Word became flesh and tabernacled among us (1:14), and in the last unit John presents Jesus identifying himself as the fulfillment of the place Jacob named Bethel ("house of God"), where he saw the angels of God ascending and descending a staircase (1:51; cf. Gen. 28:10–19). These powerfully introduced themes will be developed throughout John's Gospel, from Jesus speaking about the destruction and resurrection of the temple of his body (John 2:17–22) to the Holy of Holies–like tomb (20:12) and the giving of the Spirit to make his followers the new temple (20:22).

The second and second-to-last units (1:19–28, 35–42) present the successful testimony of the Baptist. In the first the Baptist denies that he himself is the anticipated one as he points to Jesus (1:19–28), and in the second his own disciples leave him to follow Jesus (1:35–42), showing that the Baptist's testimony was effective. As the last and culminating old covenant prophet (cf. Matt. 11:9–15), John's testimony summarizes the whole of the Old Testament, gathering everything together to shine the spotlight on the one who comes to fulfill all things.

The central component in the chiastic structure of John 1 is the Baptist's testimony about the Spirit coming down on Jesus to remain upon him (1:29–34). This central episode of John 1 recalls the glory of the Lord filling the tabernacle in Exodus 40:34 and the temple with the same in 1 Kings 8:11. The Word has tabernacled, becoming the house of God, and the Spirit has come down on him to remain.

The chiastic structure of each of the five units in John 1 supports this understanding of the way its components hang together.

Chiasms Within the Chiasm: The Five Units of John 1

With the opening words of his Gospel, "in the beginning," John signals his intention to present an account of the fulfillment of the Old Testament that reaches all the way back to its first words in Genesis 1:1. Accounting for everything John communicates in the first five verses of his Gospel puts us in mind of the final verse at its end: The world cannot "contain the books that would be written" (21:25 ESV). As we pursue the way the literary structure of John 1 enables John to communicate Old Testament fulfillment, we will not begin to exhaust all that could be said about this chapter.

As noted above, the opening words of John 2 mark a new point of departure in the unfolding of the narrative, and within the first chapter key repetitions and changes of topic join to group material into discernible units in the flow of thought in John 1. These introductory comments highlight the changes of topic, and the discussions of each unit that follow will bring out the repeated phrases and themes within the units.

Whereas John 1:1–18 is heavily concerned with the Word become flesh tabernacling among humans and revealing the glory of the only begotten Son, the following section, 1:19–28, focuses on the testimony of the Baptist in response to questions from the Jewish leadership in Jerusalem. Having clarified that he is not the expected one, the Baptist announces in 1:29–34 that he knows the identity of Jesus because of the way the Spirit descended to remain upon him. The disciples of the Baptist leave him to follow Jesus in John 1:35–42, before the chapter concludes with a passage reminiscent of Jacob and culminating with reference to his experience at Bethel in 1:43–51.

1:1–18, The Word Tabernacled in Glory

Our concern here will assume the discussion in chapters 9 and 10 and focus on the way John uses the chiastic literary structure in 1:1–18 to advance his message. This section is often referred to as the Gospel's prologue, and it does serve to introduce much that will receive fuller exposition in the ensuing narrative. As noted above, John's opening declaration of the deity of the Word (1:1–18) has a corresponding closing declaration that the divine Word has done so much it could never be contained in books, or even the world itself (21:25). Only God could do so much.

Not only is the whole Gospel of John a chiasm, or a ring, there are chiasms within the chiasm, or rings within rings. This is true of units and of units within units, and in every case meaningful conclusions can be drawn from the strategic juxtapositions. The chiastic structure of John 1:1–18 can be presented as follows:

1:1–5, The Word as God, agent of creation, life, and light
  1:6–8, John the Baptist testifies
    1:9, The true light
      1:10–11, Rejected by the world and his own
      1:12–13, Received by those born of God
    1:14, The glory of the only begotten from the Father
  1:15, John the Baptist testifies
1:16–18, The revelation of the Father in the Son

Apart from an understanding of the chiastic structure of John 1:1–18, it is hard to explain why the testimony of the Baptist would be introduced in 1:6–8 and then returned to in 1:15. Rather than imagining John haphazardly skipping around from topic to topic, saying whatever comes to mind with no organizational principle, once we understand the chiastic form we can see that he has carefully structured his statements to guide his audience through his flow of thought, with corresponding statements mutually deepening one another, forging a memorable structure that has its own admirable beauty.

This opening unit of John's Gospel begins in eternity past, in the beginning when the Word was with God prior to the making of all things (1:1–3). It ends in the last days, when the Word becomes flesh to reveal the Father (1:16–18). This encompasses the Son's career from being eternally begotten of the Father to becoming flesh to make the Father known. He was with God in the beginning, maker of all, possessor of life in himself comprising unconquerable light (1:1–5). This is the "fullness" (1:16) from which all receive grace upon grace, revealing God's own character of grace and truth (1:17; cf. Exod. 34:6–7): the only begotten who exegetes the Father (John 1:18). John speaks uniquely of the Word, the Son, in relationship with the Father at the beginning and end of this section of text, in 1:1–5 and in 1:17–18. Here the Word was with God and was God (1:1), and here the only begotten God is at the Father's side (1:18).

As noted above, apart from the chiastic structure, it is difficult to explain why John the Evangelist places the statements about John the Baptist where he does, but once we have understood the chiastic structure, we see that the introduction of the Baptist and his testimony in John 1:6–8 stands directly across from the reference to the Baptist and his testimony in 1:16. These two related units sit second and second to last, just after the beginning (1:1–5) and just before the ending (1:17–18). This structure in 1:1–18 previews the placement of the Baptist's testimony in the broader structure of 1:1–51, where we also find it in second and second-to-last positions (see above). In the prologue of the Gospel (1:1–18), the verb rendered "bear witness" appears only in these corresponding sections on the Baptist (1:7–8, 15).

John the Evangelist also sounds notes about the Baptist that he will sound about himself—the Baptist came "that all might believe through him" (1:7 ESV), and the evangelist himself writes that his audience might believe (20:31). These assertions of the purpose of prompting faith thus bracket the body of the Gospel, forming part of its wide-angle chiastic structure.

Life was in the Word, life that is the *light* of men (1:4), light that cannot be overcome by darkness (1:5). The Baptist was not that light but bore witness about it (1:8). The coming of that light into the world in John 1:9 stands third from the beginning of this section, and matching it standing third to last is the glory of the only begotten of the Father in 1:14. When these two statements are understood as being in literary relationship with each other, we see that the coming of the light into the world (1:9) is another way of describing the Word becoming flesh (1:14), which makes perfect sense in light of the fact that John earlier asserted that the life in the Word was the light of men (1:4–5). The character of the Son as the only begotten of the Father (1:14) fits the description of him as the shining light

(1:9; cf. 1:5), the glory radiating from the Father himself (1:14; cf. Heb. 1:3). These descriptors reflect the relationship of origin and equality in deity between Father and Son (see further chaps. 9 and 10 below).

At the center of John's opening chiasm in 1:1–18 we find parallel two-verse statements describing contrasting responses to the light that is life, the Word made flesh, the only begotten Son of the Father. First, in John 1:10–11, we read of how the light came into the world he made and was not known by that world, then that he came to his own people, who did not receive him. Second, in John 1:12–13, we read of those who did receive him, which amounts to believing in his name, and what he gives them in response: the right to become children of God, born anew of God himself. Thus the only begotten Son brings a new birth to those who receive him that makes them like himself, begotten of the Father (cf. 1 John 5:18).

Recognizing the chiastic literary structure of John 1:1–18 enables us to articulate a summary of the message of this section that begins from its center and works out through the corresponding sections:

> John's Gospel presents the rejection or reception of Jesus as all important, for he is the true light, radiating the very glory of the Father as the only begotten, testified to by the Baptist, as the Word made flesh, agent of creation, in whom is life and light, revealing the Father's very character more fully than even Moses experienced in Exodus 34:6–7.

1:1–5, The Word Was God

In demonstration of the aforementioned chiasms within chiasms, consider the structure of John 1:1–5. Here I present my own literal translation of John 1:1–5, with the phrases formatted in ring structure:

1:1a, In the beginning was the Word, and the Word was with God

1:1b, And the Word was God

1:2, He was in the beginning with God

1:3a, All things came about through him

1:3b, And apart from him not one thing came about that has come about

1:4a, In him was life

1:4b, And the life was the light of men

1:5, And the light shines in the darkness, and the darkness has not overcome it

With the first phrase of John's Gospel reminding readers of the Genesis 1 creation account, verse 5 further reminds John's audience that the first thing God said was "Let there be light" (Gen. 1:3 ESV). John reveals that the Word through which God spoke the world into being was actually the only begotten of the Father, who would become flesh, and that this Second Person of the Godhead was with God and was God. Standing across from the declarations that the Word was God in the beginning in 1:1b–1:2 are the affirmations that *life* was in him, life that was the light of men in 1:4. If life was in him, then the Word who was God and was with God is fully God, sharing God's own life-in-himself nature (cf. 5:26). The central statements of John 1:1–5 are the affirmations of the creator-creature distinction in 1:3. God and the Word, unconfounded persons of undivided substance, existed before anything else was made, created all that is, and nothing exists that they did not make. It is hard to imagine John more clearly affirming the absolute divinity and separate personhood of the two figures under discussion, God and the Word, the Father and his only begotten Son.

Though space constraints prevent expositions of John 1:6–8 and 1:9–13, these sections also make up chiasms within the larger chiasm, as can be shown by the formatting of my literal translation as follows:

1:6a, A man came, sent from God
1:6b, A name to him John
1:7a, He came as a witness
1:7b, That he might bear witness concerning the light
1:7c, That all might believe through him
1:8a, He was not the light
1:8b, But that he might bear witness concerning the light

1:9, The true light, which gives light to every man, was coming into the world
1:10a, He was in the world, and the world came about through him
1:10b, And the world did not know him
1:11a, He came to his own
1:11b, And his own did not receive him
1:12a, But as many as received him
1:12b, He gave to them the right to become children of God
1:12c, To those who believed in his name
1:13a, Who were not of bloods, nor of the will of flesh, nor of the will of man
1:13b, But they were born of God

1:14–18, Glory of the Only Begotten

John 1:14–18 is a most remarkable accomplishment of the Apostle, who has captured the Old Testament fulfillment God has accomplished in Christ in a stunning and surprising way. Before we consider what John has written here, we should recall the flow of events in Exodus 24–40. Moses ascended Mount Sinai, and the cloud of the glory of Yahweh covered the mountain (24:15–18). While on the mountain for forty days and nights (24:18), the Lord gave Moses the instructions for the tabernacle (chaps. 25–31), before sending Moses down from the mountain to confront the people's sin with the golden calf (chap. 32). Moses then interceded on behalf of Israel and asked to see Yahweh's glory (chap. 33), and Yahweh passed before Moses and proclaimed his name, full of grace and truth (34:6–7), before renewing the covenant (34:10–28). Moses then came down from the mountain unaware that his face shone (34:29–35). The people built the tabernacle (chaps. 35–40), and Yahweh filled it with his glory (40:34–38).

The events narrated in Exodus are directly relevant to the way John presents Christ bringing fulfillment in 1:14–18. The whole point of Israel's tabernacle was to make possible the dwelling of the holy God among the sinful people. John asserts that the Word became flesh to tabernacle among us, making it so that when Christ came in the flesh the holy God dwelled among sinners (1:14a). God's glory was seen on Mount Sinai, and when Yahweh proclaimed his name to Moses he announced himself to be the one full of grace and truth ("abounding in steadfast love and truth," Exod. 34:6), and John asserts himself as an eyewitness of the glory of the Word become flesh, the glory of the only begotten from the Father, full of grace and truth (John 1:14b).

John's statements in 1:14 and 1:17b–18 match in three ways: the mention of "grace and truth," the *seeing* of Christ's glory versus the fact that no one has ever *seen* God, and the reference to Jesus as the only begotten. No one has ever seen God (1:18), but the only begotten of the Father, the Word, has become flesh, revealing God's own full-of-grace-and-truth glory (1:14, 17b).

Inside the outer frame about the only begotten making known the full-of-grace-and-truth glory of God in 1:14 and 1:18, John mentions the testimony of the Baptist second in 1:15a, with the law given through Moses second to last in 1:17a. This stands the final old covenant prophet John across from Moses in this subunit's chiastic structure, at the center of which we find the Baptist's testimony in 1:15b, followed by the evangelist's commentary on that testimony in 1:16. What was anticipated at Sinai has become reality in Christ: God dwells among his people, showing them his glory, full of grace and truth. Here follows my literal translation of John 1:14–18 in chiastic format (with corresponding statements in italics, in bold, and underlined):

> 1:14, And the Word became flesh and tabernacled among us, and *we have seen* his glory, glory as of **the only begotten** from **the Father**, full of <u>grace and truth</u>
>
> > 1:15a, **John** bore witness concerning him, and he cried out saying
> >
> > > 1:15b, "This is he of whom I said, 'The one who comes after me has become before me, because <u>he was before me</u>'"
> > >
> > > 1:16, Because from <u>his fullness</u> we have all received grace upon grace
> >
> > 1:17a, For the law was given through **Moses**
>
> 1:17b–18, <u>Grace and truth</u> came through Jesus Christ. *No one has ever seen* God; **the only begotten** God, who is in the bosom of **the Father**, he has made him known

We can summarize the chiastic structure of John 1:14–18 as follows:

> 1:14, Glory of the only begotten full of grace and truth
>
> > 1:15a, John bore witness
> >
> > > 1:15b, John the Baptist's testimony to the deity of Christ
> > >
> > > 1:16, John the Evangelist's comment on the deity of Christ
> >
> > 1:17a, The law given through Moses
>
> 1:17b–18, The only begotten, bringer of grace and truth, makes known the Father

Spiraling into the central statements from those on the outer frames, the making known of the Father (1:18) shines forth his glory (1:14), and Christ comes as the one to whom all the prophets from Moses (1:17) to John (1:15a) bore witness. Indeed, he was before John (1:15b) in the fullness of deity (1:16a), and from that fullness flows grace upon grace (1:16b).

1:19–28, The Voice of One Crying Out in the Wilderness

As John's narrative introduction to his Gospel builds to its central section where the Spirit descends upon Jesus to remain upon him at his baptism (1:29–34), the son of Zebedee has introduced the only begotten Word made flesh to tabernacle among the people and reveal the Father's glory (1:1–18). Having hinted at the testimony of John the Baptist in 1:6–8 and 1:15, the evangelist puts the microphone in the face of the voice in the wilderness in 1:19–28.

The chiastic structure of this section centers the Baptist's self-identification as the Isaiah 40:3 voice in the wilderness preparing the way of the Lord (John 1:23). Not only does this declaration reveal who the Baptist is, it equates the coming of Jesus, whose way the Baptist professes to prepare, with the prophesied return of Yahweh to Zion. In context in Isaiah, the declaration the Baptist quotes heralds the return of Yahweh at the new exodus and return from exile to bring about the fulfillment of God living in covenant with his people.

Immediately before and after the Baptist's quotation of Isaiah 40:3 in John 1:23 we find references to the "sending" of the representatives of the Pharisees in 1:22 and 1:24. The questions posed by these sent ones precede and follow, in 1:21 and 1:25, and the two verses are worded almost identically, both containing denials that the Baptist is either Elijah or the Prophet. The verses before and after, 1:20 and 1:26, each begin with descriptions of the Baptist speaking. In the first, 1:20, he flatly declares, "I am not the Christ" (ESV). In the second, 1:26, he speaks of the one who stands among those sent to him, whom they know not, who comes after him, the strap of whose sandal the Baptist considers himself unworthy to untie. The first and last statements of this unit, 1:19 and 1:28, introduce the episode and its occasion ("And this is the testimony of John, when the Jews from Jerusalem sent priests and Levites that they might ask him, 'Who are you?'"; 1:19) and give the location and what John was doing ("These things happened in Bethany beyond the Jordan, where John was baptizing"; 1:28).

We can summarize the chiastic structure of this section on the Baptist's testimony to hostile interlocutors as follows:

- 1:19, The Baptist's testimony
  - 1:20, I am not the Christ
    - 1:21, And they asked him, "What then? Are you Elijah or the Prophet?"
      - 1:22, An answer for those who sent us
        - 1:23, I am the voice of one crying out in the wilderness
      - 1:24, They were sent from the Pharisees
    - 1:25, And they asked him, "Why then? Neither Christ, nor Elijah, nor the Prophet?"
  - 1:26–27, Among you stands . . . he who comes after me
- 1:28, John was baptizing

The Baptist continues to testify in the following two episodes; in both the focus shifts from him to Jesus in different and significant ways.

1:29–34, The Descent of the Spirit to Remain on Jesus

The eternal Word became flesh and tabernacled to show forth God's glory (1:1–18), to which John bears witness as the final old covenant prophet (1:19–28). At the baptism of Jesus, the Spirit descends upon the tabernacled Word, making him the fulfillment of the old covenant dwelling place of God, as the Baptist testifies in John 1:29–34.

The first and last verses of this unit, John 1:29 and 1:34, both contain descriptions of what the Baptist saw and said. In both cases, he sees Jesus, and in both cases, he announces a title of Jesus:

- John 1:29: "The next day he sees Jesus coming to him and he says, 'Behold, the Lamb of God, who takes away the sin of the world!'"
- John 1:34: "And I have seen and have testified that this is the Son of God."

The second and second-to-last statements in John 1:30–31 and 1:33 parallel each other in at least four ways:

1. Both contain "this is he" statements: "this is he of whom I said" in 1:30 (ESV); "this is he who baptizes with the Holy Spirit" in 1:33 (ESV).
2. In both the Baptist compares himself with Jesus: speaking of how Jesus ranks before him because he was before him in 1:30 and of how he baptizes with water but Jesus baptizes with the Spirit in 1:33.
3. In 1:31 and in 1:33 the Baptist describes his own ministry of baptizing in water.
4. The Baptist uses the same phrase in 1:31 and 1:33, saying in each verse, "I myself did not know him" (ESV).

The center of John 1:29–34 is thus John 1:32, where the Baptist testifies that he "saw the Spirit coming down as a dove from heaven, and it remained upon him [Jesus]." This information is so significant that John presents the Baptist repeating it in 1:33. The chiastic structure of John 1:29–34 can be summarized as follows:

1:29, The Baptist saw and said, "The Lamb of God"

 1:30–31, This is he; before me; baptize with water; I myself did not know him

1:32, The Spirit came down on him and remained
1:33, I myself did not know him; I baptize with water, he with the Spirit; this is he
1:34, The Baptist saw and said, "The Son of God"

The anointing of the Spirit enables the Baptist to identify Jesus as "the Son of God" in 1:34, and both the Spirit's anointing and the title point to Davidic kingship. Here we have fulfillment of the way that the Spirit left Saul and came upon David when Samuel anointed him as king (1 Sam. 16:13–14).

In the Pentateuch the only people to be anointed were the priests (Exod. 28:41; 29:7; 30:30; 40:13, 15), so the anointing of the king would have associated the king with the priesthood. There are clear temple connotations in the context of John 1–2, which include the reference to the Word "tabernacling" in 1:14; Jesus claiming he would fulfill Jacob's dream at Bethel, the house of God, in 1:51; and then Jesus speaking of the destruction and resurrection of the temple of his body in 2:19–21. In the context of these statements, the Spirit coming down on Jesus to remain on him suggests the fulfillment of God's glory filling the tabernacle in Exodus 40 and the temple in 1 Kings 8. Jesus comes as the fulfillment of the place where God would dwell in the midst of his people.

In 2 Samuel 7 David wanted to build a house for God, a temple, but God did not permit it. Instead, he promised to build David a house, a dynasty. At the center of the chiastic structure of his first chapter, John the Evangelist presents Jesus as the one who fulfills both the dynastic house God promised to David and the dwelling place David wanted to build for God.

1:35–42, The Baptist's Disciples Follow Jesus

God has descended upon the incarnate Word, fulfillment of the house of David and the house of God, by means of the Spirit's abiding presence upon Jesus (John 1:29–34). The Baptist's testimony to a hostile audience that preceded that unit (1:19–28) is now complemented by the Baptist's testimony to a receptive audience (1:35–42). The Baptist points his own disciples to Jesus (1:36), who ask where Jesus abides (1:38) and are invited by him to come and see; they see and abide with him (1:39).

The chiastic structure of John 1:35–42 can be summarized as follows:

1:35, Disciples
  1:36, Lamb of God
    1:37, The two . . . heard . . . followed Jesus
      1:38, He says to them . . . where abiding?
      1:39, He says to them . . . where he abided . . . they abided
    1:40, The two . . . heard . . . followed Jesus
  1:41, Messiah
1:42, Disciples

There are two disciples in the first and last verses of this unit: Two of the Baptist's disciples stand with him in John 1:35, and Andrew brings Peter to Jesus in 1:42. There are two titles of Jesus in the second and second-to-last verses: The Baptist identifies Jesus as the Lamb of God in 1:36, and Andrew recognizes him as Messiah, Christ, in 1:41. And then there are the remarkably parallel third and third-to-last statements in 1:37 and 1:40, both of which repeat three big ideas in the same terms: (1) there are "the two" disciples; (2) they "heard" what the Baptist said; and (3) they "followed Jesus."

The center of this unit introduces the important Johannine theme of abiding with Christ (see 8:31; 15:4). The Spirit came down on Christ to abide upon him in John 1:32, and now the disciples of the Baptist seek Jesus, addressing him as "Rabbi," asking where he abides in 1:38. In 1:39 Jesus tells them to come and see, and they see where he abides and abide there with him.

The Word who was God and was with God has come in the flesh, a man who can be described as tabernacling, as though he is a tent. He is the only begotten of the Father, and the Spirit descends upon him to remain. With him his people dwell, and the experience of these early disciples in John 1 anticipates the restoration of what was lost when Adam and Eve were driven from God's presence when they were banished from the garden.

1:43–51, The True Bethel of Whom Moses and the Prophets Wrote

After the loss of Eden, God revealed himself in special locations, such as Bethel to Jacob and Sinai to Moses, where he gave the instructions for the making of the tabernacle, later to be replaced by the temple. As Sinai and Moses figured prominently in John 1:1–18, Bethel and Jacob do the same in 1:43–51.

In the final unit of John 1 Jesus calls Philip, who in turn brings Nathanael to Jesus. In the central statement of this unit, Jesus sees Nathanael and declares, "Behold, truly an Israelite in whom there is no guile" (1:47). Whereas Jacob deceived Esau, Isaac, and Laban, in Nathanael there is no deceit. The reference to Nathanael being opposite in character to Jacob stands in conjunction with the promise that Nathanael will see "the angels of God ascending and descending upon the Son of Man" (1:51), which obviously recalls the way "the angels of God were ascending and descending upon" the flight of steps in Jacob's vision at the place he declared to be "the gate of heaven," naming it Bethel (Gen. 28:12, 17, 19).

Lest we lose our way trying to ascertain why Jesus would speak of the Son of Man in the place of Jacob's flight of steps, we must understand that Jacob's vision of a flight of steps symbolized a ziggurat-like ascent up a symbolic mountain of Yahweh, where the Lord was uniquely present. This fits with the tabernacle revealed on Mount Sinai in Exodus 25–40 as a way to regain lost access to God's presence. By means of the statement in John 1:51, Jesus presents himself as the fulfillment of places like Bethel where God revealed himself and like Sinai where he tabernacled. Jesus is the fulfillment of the house of David, he is the Word made flesh, God incarnate, the locus of God's presence on earth.

Jacob had his vision as he made his way north in flight from Esau, on his way out of the land of promise to go to his uncle Laban. In the first verse of this section, John 1:43, we read that Jesus too is going north toward Galilee, and the allusion to Bethel, site of Jacob's vision, comes in the last verse of the section, 1:51.

Just inside the outer frames are references to the disciples gathering to Jesus and the confessions of faith they make. In John 1:44–45 we read of Philip, Andrew, and Peter, before Philip finds Nathanael and tells him, "The one of whom Moses in the Law, also the Prophets, wrote, we have found! Jesus the son of Joseph, the one from Nazareth." In the corresponding statements in 1:49–50, Nathanael confesses, "Rabbi, you are the Son of God; you are the king of Israel," and Jesus promises he will see even greater things.

Several important conclusions become apparent when we allow the chiastic structure of the passage to prompt us to consider the two confessions as mutually interpretive. First, we see that the Law and the Prophets are both understood to point forward to the "son of God" who is the "king of Israel." Adam and Israel have "son of God" status in the Law, and then in the Prophets (1–2 Samuel being considered part of the Prophets) David is told that his seed will also have "son of God" status. John presents the early disciples of Jesus interpreting the "son of God" in both the Law and the Prophets as being fulfilled in Jesus. This also indicates that Adam's royal dominion (Gen. 1:26–28), the kings promised to Abraham (17:6), and other indicators of a future king of Israel, such as the blessing of Judah in Genesis 49:8–12 and the prophecies of Balaam in Numbers 22–24, all point forward to the king God promised to raise up from David's line (2 Sam. 7).

Second, John presents Philip communicating to Nathanael with an excited urgency that indicates eager expectation for this figure to arise. Not only have these people learned from the Old

Testament what to expect, they have recognized their deep need for it to be fulfilled.

Third, in addition to the way that Nathanael addressing Jesus as "Rabbi" indicates that he expects the king to be a teacher, we can observe the way that Philip describes Jesus as "son of Joseph" in John 1:45, and then Nathanael addresses him as "Son of God" in 1:49. The Word becoming flesh entails the Son of God becoming the son of Joseph.

The next two corresponding statements open with almost the exact same phrase. Whereas the ESV renders the opening phrases of John 1:46 and 1:48 in the same way, "Nathanael said to him," the verb is an aorist in 1:46 and a present in 1:48. After those nearly identical opening phrases, we have reference to Nazareth, "branch place," followed by reference to Philip in 1:46, whereas in 1:48 we have reference to Philip and then to Jesus seeing Nathanael "under the fig tree."

As noted above, at the center of this chiastic unit stands Jesus' recognition of Nathanael as an Israelite unlike the man whose name was changed from Jacob to Israel. Whereas there was guile in the "heel-catcher" (the meaning of the name Jacob), there is none in Nathanael. The chiastic structure of John 1:43–51 can be summarized as follows:

1:43, To Galilee
- 1:44–45, Philip, Andrew, Peter, Nathanael; Moses and the Prophets wrote of him
  - 1:46, Nathanael said to him; Nazareth ("branch place"); Philip
    - 1:47, Jesus knew the Israelite with no guile
  - 1:48, Nathanael says to him; Philip; under the fig tree
- 1:49–50, Nathanael: "Rabbi, Son of God, king of Israel," greater things

1:51, Bethel

Conclusion

How can we be sure that an author, John in this case, intended to create these chiastic structures? One way for an author to signal the presence of a chiasm is to repeat key terms and themes only in the corresponding sections of his chiastic structure. If he has reserved important words or significant themes for only these units, interpreters have reason to think the author intended the layout.

In addition to the matching phrases and themes we have noted in each of the five smaller chiasms of the chapter-wide chiasm, we find the same in the whole that we found in the parts. Note, too, how the structure of the smaller units helps us establish the boundaries of the larger structure.

The thematic correspondence of the chiastic structure of the whole of John 1 is manifest and significant. In only the beginning and ending units does John present Jesus as the fulfillment of *places* God inhabited in the old covenant, the tabernacle (1:14) and Bethel, house of God where angels ascended and descended (1:51). Another fascinating detail about these first and last sections of John 1 is the fact that only in these two sections of John 1 do we find the name of Moses (1:17, 45).

Similarly, the Baptist's testimony is prominent in the second and second-to-last units, both of which open by asserting the presence of John and those to whom he testifies (1:19, 35). We read of John bearing witness to the priests and Levites sent by the Jews of Jerusalem in John 1:19, and in 1:35 we read of John testifying to two of his disciples. The introduction of these characters sets the stage for the testimony the Baptist will deliver, as he identifies himself as preparing the way for the Lord to hostile interlocuters in the first (1:23; cf. 1:19–28) and points out the Lamb of God to disciples who conclude that Jesus is the Messiah in the second (1:35, 41; cf. 1:35–42). In the same way that only the first and last sections of John 1 mention Moses by name, only the second and second-to-last sections of John 1 refer to the stand-alone title Christ, at 1:20, 1:25, and 1:41.[4]

Rather than viewing John 1:19–51 as a hodgepodge of disordered reflections, when we see the chapter's chiastic structure, we appreciate more fully how 1:1–18 both introduces the whole Gospel and stands in relationship to its first chapter. We also begin to perceive the way that John has managed to communicate simultaneously that the Triune God now reveals himself as the only begotten Son, who comes from the Father and is anointed by the Spirit, and that even as the Word becomes flesh, he comes not only in fulfillment of the promise of the king from David's line but also as the fulfillment of the temple and its priesthood.

Jesus is the fulfillment of the house of David as the king from his line *and* as the tabernacling Word, the very presence of God in the midst of his people. He is the Spirit-anointed king, indwelled tabernacle, only begotten of the Father, Word made flesh come as prophet like Moses (John 1:21), Lord (1:23), Messiah-Christ (1:25, 41), Lamb of God (1:29, 36), Son of God (1:34), "of whom Moses in the Law and also the prophets wrote" (1:45 ESV), king of Israel (1:49), and Son of Man (1:51).

Questions for Reflection and Discussion

1. What impresses you most about the arrangement of the material in John 1?
2. Did you notice that just as at the end of John's Gospel, where skeptical Thomas is convinced that Jesus has been raised (20:28), near the beginning, skeptical Nathanael is convinced that Jesus is the promised one (1:49)? How do accounts like this advance the purpose of John's Gospel: that his audience might believe (20:31)?

4. We do have the proper name with the title, "Jesus Christ," at 1:17, but only in the second and second-to-last sections of John 1 does the title Christ stand by itself.

Suggested Reading

Athanasius. *On the Incarnation: De Incarnatione Verbi Dei*. Crestwood, NY: St. Vladimir's Seminary Press, 1998.

Beale, G. K. *The Temple and the Church's Mission: A Biblical Theology of the Dwelling Place of God*. New Studies in Biblical Theology. Downers Grove, IL: InterVarsity, 2004.

Morales, L. Michael. *Who Shall Ascend the Mountain of the Lord? A Biblical Theology of the Book of Leviticus*. New Studies in Biblical Theology. Downers Grove, IL: InterVarsity, 2015.

4

FROM CANA TO CANA

Beholding and Believing in John 2–4

> Here, then, is the second reason why the Word dwelt among us,
> namely that having proved His Godhead by His works,
> He might offer the sacrifice on behalf of all,
> surrendering His own temple to death in place of all,
> to settle man's account with death and free him from the
> primal transgression.
>
> —Athanasius, *On the Incarnation* §20[1]

John continues to advance his presentation of Jesus in fulfillment of Old Testament themes and expectations by means of the literary structure in John 2–4. The whole of John 2–4 comprises a wide-angle chiasm, and the subunits of the wide-angle chiasm are themselves chiastically structured. In the whole as in the parts, seeing the literary structure helps us to establish the boundaries of the units, the big ideas of the units, and the central emphases of not only the units but the whole they join to build.

1. Athanasius, *On the Incarnation: De Incarnatione Verbi Dei* (Crestwood, NY: St. Vladimir's Seminary Press, 1998), 49.

The ensuing paragraphs will preview the relationships between the discrete episodes in John 2–4, and from there we will turn to consideration of the episodes themselves.

This cycle begins and ends at "Cana in Galilee" (2:1; 4:46), with the first and second signs that John presents Jesus doing (2:11; 4:54), both of which take place on the third day (2:1; 4:43) and result in belief (2:11; 4:53). John not only enumerates these two events in relationship to each other ("first" and "second"), he reminds his readers that the second takes place where the first did: "So he came again to Cana in Galilee, where he had made the water wine" (4:46 ESV). In both cases the passage centers on the instructions given by Jesus, as a result of which the sign takes place out of view and is then reported as people experience its results (for more on the parallel nature of the first two signs, see the discussion below).

In the Old Testament the covenant made on the third day at Mount Sinai between Yahweh and Israel was like a marriage, and the breaking of the covenant and the exile of the people from the land was like a divorce (cf. Jer. 3:8). As the prophets point to the new covenant that will be made after the new exodus that will set in motion the return from exile, they speak in marital terms (see esp. Jer. 31:31–34; Hosea 2:18–20). The expected human agent who will be the new Moses for the new exodus and the bridegroom in the new covenant is the future king from David's line (Hosea 3:5). All this deepens the symbolic significance of the new wine from the water jars at the wedding on the third day at Cana.

Abraham also took Isaac up Mount Moriah to sacrifice him there on the third day (Gen. 22:4), and on the third day Hezekiah was restored to health to worship Yahweh in the temple (2 Kings 20:5). Isaac was Abraham's beloved son, and at the exodus Yahweh declares that Israel is his firstborn son (Exod. 4:22–23). The breaking of the covenant and the exile of the people from the land is like the slaying of the son, and the prophecies of the new exodus and return from exile are likened to the resurrection of the people, God's son, from the dead (Ezek. 37; Hosea 5:14–6:3).

All this deepens the symbolic significance of the raising up of the official's son to health on the third day at Cana.

What will bring about the third day salvation that entails a wedding-like new covenant? Why, the fulfillment of the Passover at the new exodus, of course, which will simultaneously bring to fulfillment expectations generated by the sacrifice of Isaac (Gen. 22), the Levitical cult that culminates in the Day of Atonement (Lev. 16), and the prophecy of the suffering servant in Isaiah 53.

John follows the account of the first sign at Cana (John 2:1–12) with one that has Jesus in Jerusalem at Passover, where he drives the animals of sacrifice out of the temple then speaks of his own death and resurrection in terms of the tearing down and rebuilding of the temple (2:13–25). In John 1 the Word made flesh tabernacled (1:14) and promised something greater than Jacob's vision at Bethel (1:51). Now in John 2 we return to this theme of Jesus fulfilling the purpose of the temple as the place where God's wrath is propitiated and sin is dealt with, the place where God is present with his people.

This is the second episode in the cycle of events recorded in John 2–4. What is the second to last?

Standing across from John 2:13–25 we find John 4:31–42, where having stated in Samaria that a time is coming and now is when worship will no longer happen in Jerusalem but in spirit and in truth (4:21–24), Jesus asserts that the fields of Samaria are white for harvest (4:35). By fulfilling the ministry of the temple (2:13–25), Jesus can call the Samaritans out of their enmity with the Jews over the place of worship (4:9, 20–26) to himself, and they recognize him as the Savior of the world (4:42).

What will the salvation brought by the world's Savior be like?

It will be like a man going from darkness (cf. 3:2) to light (3:19–21) by means of being born of the Spirit (3:6) through faith (3:15–18). It will be like a woman who has had a series of men but who has no husband being met by the bridegroom (3:29) at a well (4:6). Abraham's servant met Rebekah at a well (Gen. 24:11–28). Jacob met Rachel at a well (Gen. 29:1–12). Moses met Zipporah at a well (Exod. 2:15–21). And the new birth Nicodemus needs (John 3:1–21) comes about through the life-giving words spoken by the one who met the Samaritan woman at the well (4:4–30).

What might we expect to find at the center of a chiastic structure that begins and ends with third-day signs, water to wine at a wedding and the healing of a beloved son? A structure that has in second and second-to-last place the fulfillment of the temple in Jesus and the implications of that fact for people long estranged from the temple, people like Samaritans, and then in third and third to last an account of the necessity of the new birth by faith matched by one that features the bridegroom and the woman at the well?

At the center of this structure we find in John 3:22–4:3 the Baptist rejoicing at the bridegroom's voice (3:29) and speaking of him as the one who has the Spirit without measure (3:34).

The chiastic structure of John 2–4 can be summarized as follows:

2:1–12, First sign: third day water to wine
  2:13–25, Passover temple cleansing
    3:1–21, Nicodemus
      3:22–4:3, The Baptist and the bridegroom
    4:4–30, The Samaritan woman
  4:31–42, Samaritan harvest: rabbi, prophet, Savior of the world
4:43–54, Second sign: third day healing of a son

We proceed to consider each of these subunits in the order they appear.

2:1–12, First Sign: Third Day Water to Wine

The parallel nature of the first two signs (John 2:1–12; 4:43–54), which bracket this whole section of John's Gospel (chaps. 2–4), can be discerned by putting the two events side by side. Table 4.1 puts the two episodes side by side with corresponding elements in bold font.

Table 4.1: Two Signs on the Third Day at Cana

	John 2:1–12 (ESV)	John 4:43–54 (ESV)
Time, Place, People Involved	**On the third day** there was a wedding at **Cana in Galilee**, and the mother of Jesus was there. [2] Jesus also was invited to the wedding with his disciples.	**After the two days** he departed for Galilee. [44] (For Jesus himself had testified that a prophet has no honor in his own hometown.) [45] So when he came to Galilee, the Galileans welcomed him, having seen all that he had done in Jerusalem at the feast. For they too had gone to the feast. [46] So he came again to **Cana in Galilee, where he had made the water wine**.
Problem	[3] **When the wine ran out**, the **mother of Jesus said to him**, "They have no wine."	And at Capernaum there was **an official whose son was ill.** [47] When this man heard that Jesus had come from Judea to Galilee, **he went to him and asked him** to come down and heal his son, for he was at the point of death.
Initial Refusal	[4] And **Jesus said to** her, "Woman, **what does this have to do with me**? My hour has not yet come."	[48] So **Jesus said to** him, **"Unless you see signs and wonders you will not believe."**
Response of Faith and Dependence	[5] His **mother said to** the servants, "Do whatever he tells you."	[49] The **official said to** him, "Sir, come down before my child dies."
Creative Words of Jesus	[6] Now there were six stone water jars there for the Jewish rites of purification, each holding twenty or thirty gallons. [7] Jesus said to the servants, "Fill the jars with water." And they filled them up to the brim. [8] And he said to them, "Now draw some out and take it to the master of the feast." So they took it.	[50] Jesus said to him, "Go; your son will live." The man believed the word that Jesus spoke to him and went on his way.
Report of the Miracle	[9] When the master of the feast tasted the water now become **wine**, and did not know where it came from (though the servants who had drawn the water knew), the master of the feast called the bridegroom [10] and **said** to him, "Everyone serves the good wine first, and when people have drunk freely, then the poor wine. But you have kept the good wine until now."	[51] As he was going down, his servants met him and told him that his son was **recovering.** [52] So he asked them the hour when he began to get better, and they **said** to him, "Yesterday at the seventh hour the fever left him."
Enumeration of the Sign and Response of Faith	[11] This, the **first** of his signs, Jesus did at Cana in Galilee, and manifested his glory. And his disciples **believed** in him.	[53] The father knew that was the hour when Jesus had said to him, "Your son will live." And he himself **believed**, and all his household. [54] This was now the **second** sign that Jesus did
Time and Place	[12] **After** this he went down to **Capernaum**, with his mother and his brothers and his disciples, and they stayed there for a few days.	**when** he had come from Judea to **Galilee**.

The chiastic structure of John 2:1–12 can be described as follows:

2:1–2, Time, place, and people involved
2:3, The lack of wine
2:4–5, Jesus, his mother, and his hour
2:6–8, The wine jars and the instructions of Jesus
2:9–10, Tasting the wine; the best saved for now
2:11, First sign; glory manifested; disciples believed
2:12, Time, place, and people involved

This structure centers "the stone water jars" used for "Jewish rites of purification" and the instructions of Jesus for these to be filled and drawn from and for the product to be taken to the master of the feast (2:6–8). The symbolic significance leaps off the page. The word of Jesus calls for the filling up of the implements of the old covenant, and that same word commands that what is best be drawn from the old, transformed and made new. That this event happens on the third day at a wedding likewise evokes the significant series of events that take place on the third day in the Old Testament as well as the way that weddings point beyond themselves to God making covenant with his people.

This event does not represent the actual initiation of the new covenant that Jesus brings. He declares in John 2:4 that his hour has not yet come. When his hour comes, however, the shadows in this passage—third day, wedding, best new wine from fulfillment of the old—will be reality.

2:13–25, Passover Temple Cleansing

The first sign having been introduced in John 2:1–12, in the central statements in the ensuing passage (2:13–25) the Jews ask Jesus what sign he shows to justify his cleansing of the temple (2:18). The statements that precede and follow that central question indicate that Jesus enigmatically offers his own death and resurrection as the validating sign of his authority. In 2:17 the disciples remember the way that David said in Psalm 69:9 that zeal for God's house would consume him, and in John 2:19 Jesus answers the question about a validating sign with the declaration "Destroy this temple and in three days I will raise it." John goes on to explain that Jesus was speaking of the temple of his own body (2:21), which resumes the theme of Jesus as the fulfillment of the temple. The identification of the temple with the body of Jesus in 2:20–22 stands across from the cleansing of the temple in 2:15–16. In the process of purifying the temple physically by driving out corruption, Jesus prefigures what he will accomplish spiritually through his death and resurrection. At his death, Jesus will put an end to the ministry of the temple and its sacrificial system, all of which is anticipated as he banishes from the temple the animals necessary for sacrifice. Bracketing this narrative are the references to Jesus being in Jerusalem at Passover and what he found there in 2:13–14 and 2:23–25.

The chiastic structure of John 2:13–25 can be depicted as follows:

2:13–14, At Passover; in Jerusalem; merchants in temple
  2:15–16, Temple cleansing; do not make my Father's house . . .
    2:17, Zeal for your house
      2:18, What sign?
    2:19, Destroy this temple
  2:20–22, The temple of his body; when raised disciples believed
2:23–25, At Passover; in Jerusalem; many believed

The references to the third day in the narrative of water to wine at a wedding (2:1) and in this passage dealing with the death and resurrection of Jesus (2:20) point to the conclusion that the death and resurrection of Jesus will bring about the new covenant. That new covenant will be like a wedding, like the fulfillment of Passover, like the destruction and rebuilding of the temple. The water to wine on the third day at a wedding points to the new covenant, as does the cleansing of the temple and the prophecy of Jesus' own death and resurrection on the third day.

3:1–21, Nicodemus

The references to "signs" and "man" at the end of John 2 and beginning of John 3 (2:23, 25; 3:1–2) link Jesus' refusal to entrust himself to those who saw the signs and believed at the end of John 2 (v. 24) to Nicodemus, a "man" (3:1) who acknowledged that "no one can do these signs that you do unless God is with him" (3:2 ESV). What Jesus says to Nicodemus in response indicates both *what* the signs signify and *how* one comes to perception: "Unless one is born again he cannot see the kingdom of God" (3:3 ESV). The signs signify that Jesus brings the kingdom, the kingdom that comes by the fulfillment of the Passover and the exodus through the death and resurrection of Jesus (cf. 2:13–25) inaugurating the new covenant in fulfillment of the old (cf. 2:1–12). Those who see signs, mighty works, but do not see in them the coming of the kingdom *are not able to see* because they have not been born again. The new birth enables people to see how the signs Jesus does communicate that he brings the kingdom.

John brackets his account of the conversation Jesus has with Nicodemus on the front end with statements about how this "man" from the Pharisees came "by night" (3:1–2) and on the back end with statements about how "the light" has come into the world but "men" loved darkness rather than light, while the one who does the truth comes to the light because his works are wrought in God (3:19–21; cf. also Jesus doing signs because God is with him in 3:2). The fact that Nicodemus came to Jesus bodes well for him.

Within the outer frame are two chiasms, the first dealing with what people are "able" to do (forms of δύναμαι, "I am able," appear 6x in 3:1–11) and the new birth (8x passive forms of γεννάω, "I beget," occur in 3:1–11), the second dealing with the necessary response of faith (forms of πιστεύω, "I believe," appear 7x in 3:12–21).

The two chiasms in John 3:1–21 fall out as follows:

3:1–2a, A man from the Pharisees; Nicodemus; night
- 3:2b, We know
  - 3:3, Jesus answered and said to him, "Truly, truly I say to you"
    - 3:4, Nicodemus said to him, "How can . . ."
      - 3:5, Unless born of water and spirit
        - 3:6, What is born of the Spirit is spirit
      - 3:7–8, Thus with all born of the Spirit
    - 3:9, Nicodemus said to him, "How can . . ."
  - 3:10–11a, Jesus answered and said to him, "Truly, truly I say to you"
- 3:11b, We know
- 3:12a, You do not believe
  - 3:12b, How will you believe
    - 3:13, The Son of Man who came down from heaven
      - 3:14, As Moses lifted the serpent
        - 3:15, That all who believe might have eternal life
      - 3:16, This is the way God loved the world
    - 3:17, God sent the Son into the world
  - 3:18a, The one who believes in him
- 3:18b, The one who does not believe

3:19–21, Light came; men loved darkness

Here Old Testament fulfillments pile up on one another. In John 3:1–11 not only does the coming of the kingdom fulfill promises, the ability to see that happening results from the fulfillment of the Ezekiel 36:25–26 cleansing and renewal of the new birth, which is also like the Spirit blowing in the Ezekiel 37:1–14 resurrection of the dry bones. Those who experience the new birth are given a new ability to perceive and understand what Jesus does, and that new perception enables them to enter the kingdom (John 3:5).

Jesus presents himself to Nicodemus as the one in whom Nicodemus should believe. In John 3:12–21 Jesus identifies himself as the answer to the riddle in Proverbs 30:4–5, the one like a son of man in Daniel 7:13–14, the typological fulfillment of the bronze serpent in Numbers 21:8–9, the lifted-up suffering servant in Isaiah 52:13, and the Son of God in 2 Samuel 7:14. Speaking with the teacher of Israel (John 3:10), Jesus lets loose a flood of Old Testament allusions, presenting himself to Nicodemus as their fulfillment.

3:22–4:3, The Baptist and the Bridegroom

The central unit in the chiasm spanning John 2–4 is the one concerned with the Baptist in 3:22–4:3. The center of the center can be found in John 3:29–30, where the Baptist speaks of Jesus as the bridegroom, states his own joy at the sound of the bridegroom's voice, and asserts, "He must increase; I must decrease" (3:30).

The chiastic structure of John 3:22–4:3 can be depicted as follows:

3:22–24, Jesus and John baptizing
  3:25–26, Dispute over cleansing
    3:27–28, Receive; from heaven; witness
      3:29a, The bridegroom
        3:29b, John's joy

3:30, He must increase
3:31–32, From heaven; witness; receive
3:33–36, The one who speaks God's word
4:1–3, Jesus and John baptizing

In the first major section of John's Gospel, 1:1–51, the Baptist's testimony that the Spirit had come down upon Jesus to remain was central (1:29–34). This marked Jesus out as the fulfillment of the promises of both an anointed king and the God-indwelled tabernacle.

Now in this second major section of John's Gospel, 2:1–4:54, the testimony of the Baptist is again central. Here the final old covenant prophet points to Jesus as the bridegroom, the human agent through whom God will initiate the new covenant with his people. As in a marital covenant with a bride and groom, where the husband initiates the covenant relationship, so also the Messiah plays the role of the bridegroom in the new covenant relationship between God and his people.

The progression of characters in this sequence of John's Gospel is also interesting: Jesus first encounters Nicodemus and tells him he must be born again (3:7) to see how the signs signify that the kingdom has come (3:3) and to enter that kingdom for himself (3:5). Next the Baptist testifies that Jesus is the bridegroom (3:29) who has the Spirit without measure (3:34). Having proclaimed the good news to a Pharisee and been attested by a prophet, Jesus then encounters the Samaritan woman at the well (4:5–7) before the people of her city proclaim him the Savior of the world (4:42).

4:4–30, The Samaritan Woman

The Baptist hails Jesus as the bridegroom (3:29), and in the very next episode Jesus meets the woman at the well. This unit of John's Gospel began with a wedding (2:1–12), and now the one who initiates the new covenant meets a Samaritan outside the covenant who will be drawn near.

John positions the encounters of Jesus with Nicodemus and the Samaritan woman across from each other in the chiastic structure of John 2–4, inviting us to compare and contrast the two. We begin with an observation about a point Nicodemus and the Samaritan woman have in common: When each first encounters Jesus, neither is following him, but in different ways each is challenged to do so.

Obviously the two differ in that Nicodemus is a Jewish man and the woman is a Samaritan. Nicodemus is a man of high standing: "the teacher of Israel" (3:10), "a man of the Pharisees," and "a ruler of the Jews" (3:1). The Jews have no dealings with the Samaritans (4:9), and this woman appears to have come to the well at a time when no one else would be there because of her compromised place in society as a woman who has had five husbands, and the one she is now with is not her husband (4:16–18). As a Pharisee, by contrast, Nicodemus was almost certainly married.

With Nicodemus Jesus speaks of the new birth and faith in terms that allude to the Old Testament at many points. To the Samaritan woman Jesus offers living water (4:10), and when she indicates her desire for it, he tells her to go call her husband (4:11–16). When she says she has no husband, Jesus reveals her relationship history (4:17–18), prompting her to ask about the dispute between whether worship should happen in Jerusalem or "on this mountain" (4:19–20).

It would appear that in the same way that Nicodemus and the Samaritan woman were not following Jesus when they first encountered him, they both eventually committed themselves to doing so. The Samaritan woman, however, believes immediately, while Nicodemus only eventually comes to faith. Remarkably, John narrates the way that others also come to faith right away because of the Samaritan woman. Nicodemus, by contrast, does not bear witness to Jesus in the narrative in John 3, and no one in that narrative is depicted coming to Jesus because of his testimony. The Samaritan woman testified of Jesus to her townspeople (4:28–29), as Nicodemus later did in Jerusalem (7:50–52) and at Jesus' burial (19:39–42).

The chiastic structure of John's account of Jesus' interaction with the Samaritan woman can be depicted as follows:

4:4–7, Samaritan woman comes to the well to draw
- 4:8–9, Disciples having gone to town, Jesus speaks with Samaritan woman
  - 4:10, The gift of God, who speaks to you
    - 4:11–12, The woman says to him, "Are you greater than Jacob?"
      - 4:13–14, The living water Jesus gives
        - 4:15, The woman says to him, "Lord"
          - 4:16, He says to her, "Go call your husband"
            - 4:17a, She answers and says to him, "I have no husband"
          - 4:17b–18, He says to her, "You have spoken truly"
        - 4:19–20, The woman says to him, "Lord"
      - 4:21–24, Worship in spirit and truth
    - 4:25, The woman says to him, "I know that Messiah comes"
  - 4:26, I Am, the one who speaks to you
- 4:27, Disciples return, marvel that he was speaking with a woman

4:28–30, Samaritan woman leaves water jar at well

At that point Jesus' disciples return, and a host of Samaritans respond to the woman's testimony and come to Jesus.

4:31–42, Samaritan Harvest: Rabbi, Prophet, Savior of the World

After the Passover and the exodus from Egypt, Israel went through the wilderness, eventually making their way to the land of promise for the conquest of Canaan. The temple cleansing at the time of the Passover in John 2:13–25 foreshadows the fulfillment of what that feast celebrates. Standing across from that event in 4:31–42 we find not a conquest of Canaanites but a conversion of Samaritans.

The Samaritan woman had moved from asking if Jesus was greater than Jacob (4:12) to recognizing him as a prophet (4:19) before mentioning the coming Messiah (4:25), prompting Jesus to identify himself as such (4:26).

At the beginning of this episode Jesus' disciples are "asking him" (ESV: "urging him") to eat, addressing him as "Rabbi" (4:31). At the end the Samaritans are "asking him" (4:40, exact same phrase as in 4:31) to abide with them, confessing him to be "the Savior of the world" (4:42). At beginning and end there are time references ("meanwhile" in 4:31; "two days" in 4:40), and the food of doing the Father's work in 4:34 has been accomplished by bringing about Samaritan belief in his word in 4:41.

Inside the outer frames of the episode (4:31–34, 40–42), Jesus urges his disciples to lift up their eyes and see the fields white for harvest in John 4:35 (second position). Those white fields are identified in 4:39 as the Samaritans coming out to him because of the testimony of the woman at the well (second-to-last position).

The central statements of this unit deal with sowing and reaping (4:36–38), and it seems that here the woman at the well has sowed the seed of her confession in the ears of her countrymen, as a result of which Jesus and his disciples will reap a harvest of Samaritan believers.

The chiastic structure of the passage can be depicted as follows:

4:31–34, They asked him—disciples about food
4:35, The fields white for harvest
4:36, That sower and reaper might rejoice together
4:37, One sows and another reaps
4:38, Others labored, you entered into their labor
4:39, Many of the Samaritans believed in him
4:40–42, They asked him—Samaritans about staying (this is the Savior of the world)

When we read the portent of the fulfillment of the Passover at the temple cleansing in John 2:13–25 together with its corresponding narrative of the harvest of believers from Samaria in 4:31–42, the relationship between the two narratives suggests that when Jesus fulfills the new exodus the land of promise will be conquered through conversion, bearing the fruit of believing hearts.

4:43–54, Second Sign: Third Day Healing of a Son

The Old Testament contains prominent deliverances of beloved sons. Abraham took Isaac up the mountain to sacrifice him on the third day, and a ram was provided (Gen. 22). Elijah raised the widow's son from the dead (1 Kings 17:17–24), and Elisha performed virtually the same miracle (2 Kings 4:8–37). The 2 Kings 4 narrative has several callbacks to the Isaac narrative (see 2 Kings 4:14, 16, 17). Jesus himself will enact the fulfillment of this pattern when he, the beloved Son of the Father, is raised from the dead. But Jesus, whom John refers to as a prophet in 4:44, also enacts the fulfillment of what the prophets Elijah and Elisha typify as he raises the official's son on the third day in John 4:43–54.

The similarity of this passage to John 2:1–12 has been noted above. Like John 2:1–12, John 4:43–54 is a chiasm:

4:43–46a, When they came to Galilee where he made the water wine (first sign)

4:46b–47, Official asks him to come down and heal his son

4:48, He said then, "Unless . . ."

4:49, Come down before my child dies

4:50, Jesus says to him, "Go, your son lives"; he believed and went

4:51, While he was coming down . . . his child lives

4:52, They said then, "At the seventh hour"

4:53, The father knew at that hour his son lives and believes

4:54, This the second sign Jesus did having come to Galilee

This section opens and closes with references to Jesus "coming" "to Galilee" (4:45, 54), and there are also references to the "first sign" in 2:1–12 at beginning and end. John 4:46 refers readers back with the words "Then he came again to Cana in Galilee, where he made the water wine," and this sign is enumerated as second in relationship to the first, the turning of water to wine (2:11): "And this again the second sign Jesus did" (4:54).

As reflected in my chiastic summary above, John has varied his language for the boy, using the term "son" in second and second-to-last positions, then switching to "child" in fourth and fourth-to-last positions, with a reference to "son" in central place. Why might John employ both terms in this narrative? His reasons for using "son" are obvious: The raising of the official's "son" points beyond itself to the raising of a greater "son." Along similar lines, the inclusion of the term translated into English as "child" (παῖς) could be meant to allude to the use of the same term in the Greek translation of "servant" (Hebrew: עֶבֶד) in Isaiah 52:13 (cf. παιδίον in 53:2 and παιδεία in 53:5). Both "servants," the one in John 4 and the one in Isaiah 53, will be raised up.

Conclusion

As in John 1, where John's chiastic structure deepens our perception of his claims of Old Testament fulfillment, so in John 2–4, the literary structure heightens our appreciation of the suggestively communicative nature of the "signs" John presents Jesus doing. Here I will begin with the first and last episodes of this literary unit, move to the second and second to last, then on to the two units that frame the center, before concluding with that central testimony of the Baptist.

At a wedding, an event in which a covenant is solemnized, on the third day, when the wine has run out, Jesus instructs that jars used for old covenant purification rites should be filled with water, and he changes that water into wine. This subtly depicts the way that the old covenant has run its course, the way that Jesus will bring what is best from it, and the way that the new covenant will be inaugurated on the third day.

Standing across from the first sign is the second, when again on the third day Jesus enacts fulfillment of the way that Elijah and Elisha raised sons from the dead, and simultaneously the narrative anticipates the way that Jesus himself, beloved Son and servant of the Lord, will be raised up on the third day. The wedding and the resurrection both took place at Cana, and the geographical location joins the similar structure of the two narratives to link the events. Their fulfillments will likewise happen in the same place on the third day.

John will narrate several Passover feasts in his Gospel, at the first of which Christ cleanses the temple. In keeping with the pattern so far, the actions of Jesus subtly point to the way he will bring Old Testament expectation to its fulfillment. Across the Old Testament the prophets point to the past to explain the present and predict the future. What God did for his people at the exodus is what he will do for them when he accomplishes their future deliverance.

At this first Passover in the Gospel of John, the one hailed by the Baptist as the Lamb of God drives animals of sacrifice away from the temple. And when asked what sign he gives to show that he has the authority required for such action, he speaks of his own death and resurrection as the destruction and rebuilding of the temple. In the same way that zeal for God's house consumed David, the zeal that Jesus feels for God's house will consume him. The house for which Jesus feels consuming zeal is not only the temple he has cleansed (the building) but the temple of the Spirit that he will cleanse (the people). Jesus will die for his people, putting an end to the need for sacrifices at the Jerusalem temple. When he was raised from the dead his disciples remembered and understood.

Standing across from the temple cleansing at Passover in John's chiastic structure of chapters 2–4 is the "harvest" of the Samaritan converts. Israel left Egypt after the first Passover to make their way through the wilderness to conquer the land of Canaan. After the temple-cleansing intimation of the fulfillment of Passover, John intimates a fulfillment of the conquest, not by means of the death of the inhabitants of Canaan but by their conversion. When John depicts Jesus speaking of the Samaritans ripe for conversion as the fields being white for harvest, it is as though the land is bearing fruit, and the disciples enter into the labor of the ingathering.

The conversation with Nicodemus in John 3 brims with Old Testament fulfillment. Jesus presents himself to Nicodemus as the one doing signs that mean the kingdom of God has come, the kingdom that will be entered by those whose bodies have been sprinkled with clean water, whose hearts of stone have been removed and replaced with hearts of flesh. Jesus speaks to Nicodemus as the one who gives the new heart by means of a new birth with a sprinkling of clean water and the impartation of the Spirit. Not only does Jesus bring about that Ezekiel 36 new heart, he brings the Ezekiel 37 wind blowing where it pleases, sound heard but source unknown. When asked how these things can be, Jesus reveals himself as the answer to the riddling question about who ascends and descends in Proverbs 30:4, as the Daniel 7:13 son of man, as the Isaiah 52:13 lifted-up servant, typological fulfillment of the bronze serpent uplifted in the wilderness (Num. 21:8–9), source of life eternal no snake can take.

Standing across from that conversation with Nicodemus is the one with the woman at the well, and this with the one who has just been hailed by the Baptist as the bridegroom. Jesus meets the woman from Sychar at a well, where wives were repeatedly found in the Old Testament. She herself is not the gentile bride of Christ, but here again the things John presents Jesus doing, the events he narrates, suggest the way the blessing of Abraham will come to the gentiles in Christ Jesus (cf. Gal. 3:14). When Jesus offers the woman living water, it is as though he has held out peace to the far off and the near, as the Father seeks those who will worship no longer in Jerusalem or on the mount in Samaria but in spirit and truth. Jesus brings salvation for Pharisees like Nicodemus and for Samaritans like this unnamed woman. All the families of the earth blessed in the seed of Abraham indeed.

As in John 1 so in John 2–4: The testimony of the Baptist stands in central position. Whereas in John 1 he identified Jesus as the one on whom the Spirit came down to abide, so in John 3 he explains that he has the joy of the friend of the bridegroom. Jesus, the one who must increase as John decreases, comes to inaugurate the new covenant with God's people. Here again there is no literal human marriage into which Jesus will enter with a particular human woman. He is not the bridegroom in that sense. The language of the wedding points to the covenant God will make with his people, with Jesus as the human agent through whom it will be ratified. As the Baptist saw the Spirit come down on him to remain in John 1, so in John 3 Jesus has the Spirit without measure from the Father.

Questions for Reflection and Discussion

1. Authors reveal character by showing what people say and do, and also by showing how others respond to them. What stands out to you most from John's characterization of Jesus in chapters 2–4 of John's Gospel?
2. John tells his audience that his purpose in writing was that people might believe that Jesus is the Christ (20:31). What strikes you as most compelling about his presentation of Jesus in these narratives?

Suggested Reading

Dempster, Stephen G. *Dominion and Dynasty: A Biblical Theology of the Hebrew Bible*. New Studies in Biblical Theology. Downers Grove, IL: InterVarsity, 2003.

Dempster, Stephen G. "From Slight Peg to Cornerstone to Capstone: The Resurrection of Christ on 'the Third Day' According to the Scriptures." *The Westminster Theological Journal* 76 (2014): 371–409.

Dempster, Stephen G. "The Servant of the Lord." In *Central Themes in Biblical Theology: Mapping Unity in Diversity*, edited by Scott J. Hafemann and Paul R. House. Grand Rapids: Baker Academic, 2007.

5

LIFE FROM THE DEAD

In Public, Among Crowds, at Feasts in John 5–11

He prays, yet he hears prayer.
He weeps, yet he puts an end to weeping.
He asks where Lazarus is laid—he was man;
yet he raises Lazarus—he was God.

—Gregory of Nazianzus,
Oration 29.20[1]

The two central blocks of material in John's Gospel stand in chapters 5–11 and 12–17. Each large unit is distinctively bracketed and internally consistent, and the two are manifestly different from each other. In John 5:25 Jesus declares that "an hour is coming, and is now here, when the dead will hear the

1. Gregory of Nazianzus, *On God and Christ: The Five Theological Orations and Two Letters to Cledonius*, trans. Frederick Williams and Lionel R. Wickham, Popular Patristics Series (Crestwood, NY: St. Vladimir's Seminary Press, 2002), 87–88.

voice of the Son of God, and those who hear will live" (ESV). Then in John 11:43 that very thing happens when Jesus "cried out with a loud voice, 'Lazarus, come out'" (ESV). The material this resurrection bookend surrounds is consistent with itself in that the events are set at feasts: an unnamed feast in John 5 (v. 1), Passover in John 6 (v. 4), Tabernacles in John 7–9 (7:2), Dedication in John 10 (v. 22), and then Passover again in John 11 (v. 55). The modern chapter divisions reflect blocks of material in which Jesus does and says things in public (note how the same phrase introduces 5:1; 6:1; and 7:1; cf. 10:22). In John 5 Jesus heals the man at the pool and then teaches. In John 6 he feeds the five thousand, walks on water, then teaches. In John 7–8 he teaches publicly at Tabernacles, offering himself as the water source and the light of the world, before healing the man born blind in John 9. He then presents himself as the good shepherd in John 10, before raising Lazarus from the dead in John 11.

If we compare John 5–11 with John 12–17, we find the latter portion bracketed by Jesus announcing that the hour has come for the Son to be glorified (12:23; 17:1). Whereas John 5–11 took place in public, among the crowds, at several different feasts, John 12–17 takes place in private, with only the disciples, at the final Passover. Reflecting the difference between the settings, the kinds of things John presents Jesus saying in John 5–11 differ markedly from the kinds of things he says in John 12–17, and yet the voice is consistent throughout.

Once we see the parameters of John 5–11, we are in position to consider the way that here John presents Jesus speaking life-giving words of resurrection power in John 5 and 11, presenting himself as manna from heaven and water from the rock in John 6–7, which stands across from him giving sight to the blind as the good shepherd in John 9–10, with the whole centering on his self-assertion as the light of the world in John 8. Literary structure continues to advance John's claims of Old Testament fulfillment. The chiastic structure of John 5–11 can be depicted as follows:

John 5:1–47, The dead will hear the voice of the Son of God and live

John 6:1–71, I am the bread of life

John 7:1–52, If anyone is thirsty, let him come to me and drink

John 8:12–59, I am the light of the world

John 9:1–41, Sight for the man born blind

John 10:1–42, I am the good shepherd

John 11:1–44, Lazarus, come forth

Resurrection hope pulses through the pages of the Old Testament. Such hope is necessary because dying man died in the day he ate of the fruit of the tree of the knowledge of good and evil (Gen. 2–3). Not only did Adam, God's son, die, Israel, God's son, also died when he broke the covenant like Adam and was driven from God's presence (2 Kings 25). Banished from the clean realm of life to the unclean realm of the dead, the nation was a valley of dry bones in exile, awaiting the prophetic word and the coming of the Spirit like the sound of wind to make the bones rattle and live (Ezek. 37). Jesus hinted that he would bring the spiritual side of this new life to Nicodemus in John 3, but in John 5 he points to bodily resurrection and then in John 11 accomplishes it. As with the wedding at Cana and the healing of the official's son, however, the resurrection of Lazarus is but an anticipation of the fulfillment of the Old Testament resurrection hope that Jesus will bring.

In addition to the Old Testament likening the restoration of the people to the presence of God to resurrection from the dead, the future salvation is also likened to the exodus from Egypt (e.g., Isa. 11:11, 15–16). God commanded Israel to celebrate the Passover yearly so that each new generation could rehearse the events of the exodus and enter the narrative for themselves (Exod. 12–13).[2]

2. See esp. Exod. 13:8 (ESV): "What the Lord did for me when I came out of Egypt."

The Feast of Tabernacles likewise celebrated the way that God provided for Israel through the wilderness as they dwelled in booths, eating manna from heaven, drinking water from the rock, led by the pillar of fire (Lev. 23:42–43). In his uniquely evocative way, John presents Jesus as the one who brings all this to fulfillment. Jesus is not only the new Moses who leads the people at the new exodus, but he himself is the new manna in that he is the bread of life in John 6 (v. 35). Moreover, Jesus will give something better than water from the rock to those who depend upon him for their passage through the wilderness: To those who thirst and go to him to drink he promises to give the Holy Spirit (7:37–39). And the new people who enter into the new covenant at the new exodus will not follow a new pillar of fire but the one who is the light of the world (8:12).

Isaiah prophesied that "the eyes of the blind shall be opened" and that "the lame man [will] leap like a deer" (Isa. 35:5–6 ESV). Jesus heals the lame man at the Pool of Bethesda in John 5, and then in John 9 he gives sight to the man born blind. Ezekiel prophesied that the Lord himself would shepherd his people through David the prince (Ezek. 34:11–24), and in John 10 Jesus presents himself as the good shepherd.

The literary structure advances the claim of fulfillment, so in this chapter we explore John's theology by "reading this with that," the "thises" and "thats" being the corresponding pediments in the chiastic structure: John 5 and 11 together under the heading "Giver of Life"; John 6 and 10 under the heading "New and Better Moses"; John 7 and 9, "Your Eyes Shall See Your Teacher"; and in central position John 8, "The Life Was the Light of Men."

Giver of Life: John 5 and 11

The contents of John 5 are distinguished from what came before and what comes after by differences of time and place. Whereas the final episode in John 4 took place in Cana in Galilee (4:46),

John 5:1 places the events of the chapter "after this" at "a feast" for which "Jesus went up to Jerusalem" (ESV). It seems that the healing narrated in John 5:1–18 is to be understood as the context for interpreting what Jesus says about how he can do nothing of himself in 5:19–30 and how he has valid testimony that the Father sent him in 5:31–47. John 6 opens like John 5, with the words "after this," followed by a new location, "Galilee" (6:1), and then we shortly read that "the Passover, the feast of the Jews, was at hand" (6:4 ESV). All this indicates that we should interpret John 5 as a healing event followed by comments from Jesus that are meant to be understood alongside that healing.

5:1–47, The Lame Man Healed on the Sabbath

The sequence of events and statements in John 5 prompt the interpreter to ask a number of questions: What does the healing of a lame man signify? To what was the Sabbath rest intended to point? Does God observe the Sabbath? Thus far the first section of the chapter, where John presents Jesus healing the man at the Pool of Bethesda on a Sabbath in 5:1–18.

More questions arise when we continue into what John then presents Jesus saying in 5:19–30, such as: Can we get to the bottom of the idea that the Son can do nothing of himself (5:19, 30), or does that go all the way down forever?[3] Has John presented Jesus saying these things about giving life to the dead (5:21) and having life in himself (5:26) right after the healing of the lame man on the Sabbath because these ideas are connected? And is there a relationship between the healing, the Sabbath, the resurrection, the judgment Jesus says the Father has given him (5:22, 27), and the honor the Father wants shown to the Son (5:23)?

3. Here I allude to an illustration I once heard Thomas R. Schreiner use in a sermon that went something like this: A little boy asks his father, "What holds the world up, Daddy?" The father replies, "The world sits on the back of a giant turtle." To which the son asks, "What holds the turtle up, Daddy?" The father answers, "It's turtle all the way down."

As we continue through John 5, in 5:31–47 the focus of the comments John presents Jesus making shifts to what counts as testimony to the idea that the Father sent Jesus. Here Jesus insists that "the works" the Father "has given" him to do bear witness (5:36). The "works" in view would seem to include the healing of the lame man on the Sabbath in 5:1–18, the raising of the dead and giving them life in 5:21, the "giving" of judgment to the Son in 5:22, and the "gift" of life in himself and authority to judge in 5:26–27.

The literary structure of John 5 puts us in position to think well about each of the questions raised in the past three paragraphs. The narrative of the healing, John 5:1–18, is a self-contained chiasm, as are the two blocks of teaching that follow in 5:19–30 and 5:31–47. The reference to the way the "works" bear witness to Jesus in the third unit (5:31–47) hearkens back to the healing in the first (5:1–18), indicating that here we have an A-B-A′ structure that centers on the Son doing what the Father does to save those who hear the Son's word and believe (5:19–30):

5:1–18, The Sabbath healing at the Pool of Bethesda
    5:19–30, The Son does what the Father does
5:31–47, Testimony to Jesus

The Sabbath healing prompts the controversy that ensues in John 5, which results in the statement "the Jews were seeking all the more to kill him" (5:18 ESV).

5:1–18, The Sabbath Healing at the Pool of Bethesda

The structure of John 5:1–18 highlights the controversy-causing element of the story. The central statements in the chiastic structure are found at 5:9b–10, "Now it was a Sabbath, so the Jews said to the one who had been healed, 'It is the Sabbath, and it is not right for you to take up your mat.'" This central statement is surrounded by references to the man being "made well" and to

Jesus telling the man "take up your mat and walk" (5:8–9, 11–12). As we move out from the center of the ring, in the next concentric circle we find the healed man communicating his ignorance—this applies to his vain superstition about the pool in 5:7 and to his lack of knowledge of who Jesus is in 5:13. In the ring outside the healed man's words are the words of Jesus, who asks him if he wants to be healed in 5:6 and tells him to stop sinning lest something worse happen to him in 5:14.

If the intro to this episode is suggestive, its outro is explosive. The setup (intro) for the healing in John 5:1–5 includes references to "the blind, the lame, the withered" in 5:3, recalling the promise that just these would be healed in Isaiah 35:5–6. This is matched by the episode's aftermath (outro), in which "the Jews were seeking Jesus, because he was doing these things on the Sabbath" in John 5:16. Jewish opposition to Jesus lights the fuse, but the words of Jesus supply the TNT for the blast: "Jesus answered them, 'My Father is working until now, and I am working'" (5:17 ESV). We are not at all surprised to read in 5:18, "On account of this the Jews were seeking all the more to kill him, because not only was he loosing the Sabbath, but he was also calling God his own Father, making himself equal with God." The chiastic structure of the passage can be depicted as follows:

- 5:1–2, Feast in Jerusalem, Sheep Gate, Pool of Bethesda
  - 5:3–5, Among the sick a man invalid for thirty-eight years
    - 5:6, Jesus asks the man if he wants to be healed
      - 5:7, The man explains the pool
        - 5:8, Jesus: "Rise, take up your mat, and walk"
          - 5:9a, Immediately healed and obeyed
            - 5:9b, That day was a Sabbath
            - 5:10, The Jews object

5:11, The one who healed him told him to
5:12, The Jews ask who told him rise and walk
5:13, The man does not know who healed him
5:14, Jesus tells the man to sin no more lest something worse . . .
5:15, The man proclaimed to the Jews that Jesus healed him
5:16–18, Jews seeking Jesus for Sabbath healing and making himself equal with God

John presents the words of Jesus in John 5:17 followed by his own comment on them in 5:18. This indicates that John means for his audience to understand the conclusions he himself has drawn from the actions and words of Jesus, which in turn means we can begin to answer the questions posed above. We begin with what Moses seems to have intended to communicate by depicting God resting on the seventh day and making it holy in Genesis 2:1–3. The point is not that God had exhausted his powers through the work of the creation week and needed refreshment. Rather, as the great king of creation God had completed his cosmic temple and took up rest in the house he built to enjoy with those who bear his image (cf. Isa. 66:1). That is to say, observance of the Sabbath as mandated in the Mosaic law points *back* to the experience of the presence of God in the garden of Eden and *forward* to the enjoyment of God's presence in the new heaven and new earth.

Adam and Eve brought death into the world through sin, and because of their rebellion and resulting defilement, they were driven out of God's presence in the clean realm of life into the unclean realm of the dead. All manner of sickness, infirmity, weakness, and bodily malfunction entered the world because of God's judgment against sin. God created the world very good (Gen. 1:31), but because of sin it was subjected to futility (Rom. 8:20).

The lameness of the man at the Pool of Bethesda, then, is to be understood in this imaginary. Had there been no sin, the man would not have been lame. The lame man's weakness (John 5:5) testifies to the fallenness of the world, to man's banishment from God's presence. The healing of the lame man, then, points to the removal of the effects of the curse, which implies the removal of the grounds for the curse. For this man to be healed is for him to be made fit to enter the presence of God.

In other words, for this man to be healed is for this man to be made fit to celebrate the Sabbath, the whole point of which was to recall and anticipate the enjoyment of God's presence. The Jewish opponents of Jesus have failed to understand the Sabbath, failed to understand the healing, failed to recognize Jesus, and thus failed to know God.

For the Jews opposed to Jesus, the *rest*oration of a man to a physical state that would enable him to engage in the essence of Sabbath rest was judged not for what it was—the achievement of Sabbath—but as a violation (cf. 7:23–24).

These Jews opposed to Jesus fail to understand what the Sabbath is, fail to see how Jesus has made the lame man fit for it, and fail to perceive that God has not been keeping Sabbath but has been always being who he is, the one who upholds all things by the word of his power (cf. Heb. 1:3). God has not been ceasing from that activity on the seventh day, and thus the world has held together. And Jesus is included in the identity of the God who has been always at work bearing all things along since the foundation of the world. Thus Jesus asserts: "My Father is working until now, and I am working" (John 5:17 ESV). To the consternation of his opponents, Jesus informs them that God does not keep Sabbath but works.

John puts this plainly in his interpretive gloss in 5:18, "Jesus was loosing Sabbath." He was doing that, announcing that the time in which the requirements of the old covenant was active was coming to an end (cf. "an hour is coming and is now here" in 4:23

and 5:25), and he was also including himself in the identity of God: "He was calling God his own Father, making himself equal with God" (5:18 ESV).

The Sabbath points forward to the enjoyment of God's presence in the new heaven and new earth, and the healing of the lame points to the resurrection of the body and its restoration to its created function. The resurrection is exactly what Jesus goes on to address in John 5:19–30.

5:19–30, The Son Does What the Father Does

In focus here is the contribution of the literary structure of John 5 to our understanding of the relationship between the healing in 5:1–18 and the two blocks of teaching in 5:19–30 and 5:31–47. John's A-B-A′ structure indicates that the healing in 5:1–18 (A) is the primary witness-bearing work in 5:31–47 (A′), while the import of the healing is drawn out in the chapter's central teaching block in 5:19–30 (B).

The issues that prompt the words of Jesus in John 5:19–30 are that: (1) Jesus has announced himself to be equal with God (5:18); (2) Jesus asserted that the Father continues his work, apparently in disregard of the Sabbath, and so the Son does likewise (5:17); and (3) all this was triggered when Jesus restored a man's whole body on a Sabbath (5:9–10, 16; cf. 7:23). The comments that Jesus makes in John 5:19–30 have a clearly mirrored character: beginning and ending with identically worded statements about how the Son can do nothing from himself (5:19 and 5:30); moving to second and second-to-last sections in which Jesus asserts—with the same phrasing—that just as the Father has life and gives it to the dead, so the Son has life and gives it to the dead, and that the Father has given judgment to the Son (5:20–23 and 5:25–29); and at the center asserting that the one who hears the Son and believes the one who sent him has eternal life and does not come into judgment but has passed from death to life (5:24). The chiasm can be depicted as follows:

5:19, The Son is not able to do anything from himself
    5:20–23, Resurrection; judgment; honor
        5:24, The one who hears and believes has life
    5:25–29, Resurrection; judgment; rewards
5:30, I am not able to do anything from myself

Consider the logic of the flow of thought in this passage. Jesus heals the man on the Sabbath, upsetting the Jews, who fail to understand the way he has fulfilled the Sabbath and instead think he has violated it. To address their concern, Jesus explains that the Father is working and he is too, which only exacerbates the problem, to the point of making them ready to execute him. Now he has not only violated the Sabbath but made himself equal with God. Jesus patiently proceeds to explain trinitarian reality to these who would execute God.

To justify his action of healing the man on the Sabbath, Jesus asserts that he has not performed his own will by acting from himself (5:19a, 30a) but done what he *saw* the Father doing (5:19b), and what he *heard* from the Father he judged appropriate (5:30b). What the Son saw and heard from the Father, then, enabled the Son to know the Father's will (5:30c), with the result that Jesus can say: "Whatever he [the Father] does, these things the Son likewise does" (5:19c). In John 5:19 and 5:30, then, Jesus has elaborated on the assertion in 5:17, "My Father is working until now, and I am working" (ESV). Jesus healed on the Sabbath not because he acted impulsively on his own but because he saw and heard the Father, knew his will, and did the will of the one who sent him.

As Jesus continues to explain himself to his Jewish opponents in John 5:20–23 and 5:25–29, he seems to move from the source of his action (5:19 and 5:30) to the purpose and meaning not only of the healing but of the Sabbath itself. As we have noted, the Sabbath was about the remembrance of Eden in anticipation of the New Jerusalem, and only the whole can enter God's presence. The healing of the man on the Sabbath signifies God's plan to bring Sabbath observance to fulfillment when resurrected and glorified worshipers relish the Triune God who loved and saved them and equipped them to enjoy glory. And thus Jesus says the Father loves him and shows him what he does, that he might do greater things, to cause his disciples to marvel, in John 5:20. This is why Jesus proceeds to say that as the Father raises the dead and gives them life, so the Son gives life to whom he wills in 5:21. By healing the lame man on the Sabbath, the Son has done what the Father does when he raises the dead and gives them life in his presence.

To these his own to whom he has come who have not received him (cf. 1:11), who in fact are now ready to kill him (5:18), Jesus asserts that the Father has entrusted all judgment to the Son (5:22), "that all might honor the Son as they honor the Father" (5:23a). In fact, Jesus goes on to say, "The one who does not honor the Son does not honor the Father who sent him" (5:23b).

Jesus restates the big ideas in John 5:20–23, with some developments, in 5:25–29. Here again are the themes of Father and Son raising the dead (5:21, 25, 28), of the Son acting just as the Father does (5:21, 26), and of the Father giving the Son authority to judge (5:22, 27). As we hear the music of the variations on these themes, however, we do get new information. First, in 5:25 Jesus speaks of the dead hearing the voice of the Son of God, indicating that he will summon the dead from their graves with a shout, which he does for Lazarus in John 11. Just as the Son will summon the dead from their graves by his call, so his word, "Take up your mat and walk" (5:8), summoned the lame man out of weakness into strength.

Second, in the "as the Father so the Son" statement in 5:26, Jesus speaks of the Father having life in himself and granting the same to the Son. Such a gift takes us deep into the mystery of the Trinity, with the Son eternally begotten of the Father. If the Son is God, there never can have been a time when the Father was not granting the Son to have life in himself. The Son was not created but begotten, and this happened not in time but always (cf. 1:4).

And third, in John 5:27 this judgment the Father has given to the Son decides eternal destiny. Jesus explains in 5:29 that those who have done good will go into the resurrection of life, while those who have done evil enter the resurrection of judgment. And the central statements in this chiastic structure (5:24) define the doing of good and evil that determines whether one rises to life or condemnation.

In John 5:24 Jesus solemnly tells these who think righteousness requires killing him that in reality righteousness results from hearing his word and believing his Father. Those who hear and believe do not enter judgment but pass beyond death into life. We should not fail to observe the contrast between Jesus and his opponents. He stands before them as a restorer of life, healer of the lame, who promises to summon the dead from their graves. They, on the other hand, seek to put the life-giver to death. Rightly will he tell them that they are of their father the devil at the center of this section (8:44).

There is a literary relationship between the first and last sections of John 5 in that the healing in 5:1–18 testifies to Jesus in 5:31–47, but there is also a logical progression in this chapter. The Jews think Jesus has violated the Sabbath in 5:1–18, but he explains that he has only done what the Father does in 5:19–30, and then in 5:31–47 he points to testimony that supports his claims.

5:31–47, Testimony to Jesus

In the same way that Jesus has not acted from himself (5:19, 30), his assertions about himself neither arise from his own self-invention nor stand on their own (5:31). Thus in John 5:31–47 Jesus points to those who testify to the truth of his claims. The most significant witness on his behalf is the one Jesus alludes to first, the Father (5:32). He will elaborate on the idea that the Father bears witness to him (5:37), but it seems that he mentions him first somewhat cryptically ("There is another who bears witness about me," 5:32 ESV) because the Father's testimony comes through in the others Jesus will mention: the Baptist, the works, the Scriptures, and Moses.

Jesus names prophets near the beginning and near the end, with the Baptist coming in the first few statements and Moses standing in the last (5:33, 45–47). In second and second-to-last positions are statements that begin with the words "I do not receive . . . from man/men," and what is not received is testimony in the first instance (5:34) and glory in the second (5:41). The Baptist is likened to a "lamp" that was "burning" and "shining" and giving "light" (5:35), and these references seem to correspond to the three mentions of "glory" (5:41–44). The Baptist's light was to help people see Jesus, that the glory of God is at work in him, but the opponents of Jesus have ultimately rejected not only the shining lamp but the brightness of glory.

In John 5:36 Jesus points to a greater testimony than that of the Baptist, and in doing so he brings together the first two sections of the chapter, asserting that the "works" the Father has given him testify. One of the works is certainly the healing of the man on the Sabbath (5:1–18), and others surely include the resurrection of the dead and the judgment (5:19–30), things the Father gave the Son to do, which he claims to have seen and heard from the Father. In addition to the "works" that testify in 5:36, Jesus comes right out and says that the Father testifies concerning him in 5:37a. This unit, 5:36–37a, corresponds to 5:39–40, where the Scriptures are said to testify concerning Jesus. Both sections contain a phrase built of a form of the verb "testify / bear witness" complemented by the prepositional phrase "concerning me." It seems fitting, too, that the biblical works and the Father stand across from the Scriptures as joint witnesses to Jesus.

At the center of the chiastic structure of John 5:31–47 stands 5:37b–38. Jesus has just asserted that the Father bears witness to him in 5:37a, when he proceeds to tell his opponents:

> You have never heard his voice nor seen his form,
> and his word you do not have abiding in you,

because the one whom he sent,
in this one you do not believe. (5:37b–38)

Jesus has claimed to have both seen (5:19) and heard (5:30) from the Father, and John presents him as the Word made flesh (1:14). Jesus will urge his disciples to abide in him by having his word abide in them (8:31–32; 15:7). These his opponents, however, have rejected him, the Word sent by the Father. The chiastic structure of John 5:31–47 can be summarized as follows:

5:31–33, True testimony; the Baptist
  5:34–35, I do not receive testimony from man
    5:36–37a, The works and the Father testify
      5:37b–38, You know not God
    5:39–40, The Scriptures testify
  5:41–44, I do not receive glory from man
5:45–47, True accusation; Moses

John advances his message by means of his literary structure. What better way to signal to his audience that the healing of the lame man on the Sabbath points to resurrection from the dead than to align John 5, in which Jesus says that the dead will hear the voice of the Son of God and live (5:25), across from John 11, in which that very thing happens (11:43–44)?

11:1–44, Lazarus Raised

We must first establish the boundaries of the sections before we can discuss their relationship to one another. The grammatical construction that opens John 11:1 (ἦν δέ), with the mention of Bethany, appears again at 11:18. This and other features of the text, not least the mention of the Jews in 11:19 and again in 11:36, indicate that the first two units of John 11 span verses 1–17 and verses 18–37. Once these units are established by the repeated phrase at 11:1 and 11:18, we can see that each has a self-contained continuity of theme: in the first, 11:1–17, Lazarus's predicament is introduced, and Jesus discusses it with his disciples; in the second, 11:18–37, Jesus arrives in Bethany and interacts first with Martha then Mary. The third unit focuses on Jesus raising Lazarus in 11:38–44.[4]

John 5 and 11 are thus inverted mirror images of each other. Whereas there are three units in John 5, a healing followed by two blocks of teaching, there are also three units in John 11, two blocks of dialogue between Jesus and his followers, followed by the resurrection of Lazarus. As we saw John 5 to have an A-B-A′ structure, so also John 11 has an A-B-A′ structure:

11:1–17, The life was the light of men
  11:18–37, I am the resurrection and the life
11:38–44, The dead hears the voice of the Son of God

The first three sections of John 11 all center on the words of Jesus, and each points back to the beginning of this section of the Gospel, John 5. Here we will focus our attention on the literary structure of the unit and the way it calls back to John 5. The strongest and most obvious connection between John 5 and John 11 is the way that what Jesus says will happen in 5:25, "The dead will hear the voice of the Son of God, and those who hear will live" (ESV), is exactly what takes place in 11:43–44 when he summons Lazarus from the tomb.

11:1–17, The Life Was the Light of Men

Just as John 5:3 spoke of "a multitude of the sick" and 5:5 described a man thirty-eight years "in his sickness" (ESV: "invalid[s]"), Lazarus is described as "sick" (ESV: "ill[ness]") five times in John

4. As discussed in chap. 2 above, the final two sections of John 11, vv. 45–53 and 54–57, stand at the center of John's Gospel with the first two sections of John 12, vv. 1–8 and 9–19.

11:1–6. Another interesting point of contact that reaches further back than John 5 to the last episode of John 4 comes in the way that once Jesus heard that Lazarus was sick in John 11:6, "then indeed he remained in that place two days." The phrase here closely matches the way that right before the raising of the official's son, in John 4:40 Jesus "remained there two days." In both cases, "after" the two days Jesus restores life (4:43; 11:7), implicitly placing both the healing of the official's son and the raising of Lazarus on the third day.

The central statements of John 11:1–17 entail the disciples reminding Jesus in 11:8 that "the Jews were just now seeking to stone you" (ESV), which recalls not only the immediately preceding events (10:31, 39) but also those at the beginning of this section of the Gospel (5:16–18). Jesus responds in 11:9–10 with words about walking in the day as opposed to walking in the night (cf. Eccles. 2:13–14), explaining that the one who walks in the day does not stumble "because he sees *the light of* this *world*" (John 11:9 ESV, emphasis mine).

The phrase "light of the world" exactly matches the use of the same in John 8:12, being followed in 11:9 with the demonstrative pronoun "this." (English translation requires its placement in a different position, but the phrases are exact matches in the original Greek.) It is not uncommon for chiastic structures to have points of contact with their centers at beginning and end. John 1:4 states, "In him was life, and the life was the light of men" (ESV). In John 5:26 Jesus speaks of the Father granting the Son to have life in himself. In 8:12 he asserts himself the light of the world. And in 11:9 that phrase, "light of the world," appears again.

What Jesus says about those who walk "in the night" in 11:10 is also fascinating. It recalls the way that Nicodemus came to Jesus at night in 3:2 and portends the way Judas went out "and it was night" in 13:30. Jesus, who asserted himself to be the light of the world in 8:12, says in 11:10 that the one who walks in the night "stumbles, because the light is not in him" (ESV). This recalls John 5:38, where Jesus said, "And you do not have his word abiding in you" (ESV). As there so here: The words of Jesus point beyond unbelievers lacking "the word" or "light" within themselves to the one John's Gospel names as both, Jesus himself.

11:1–2, Lazarus sick; Mary and Martha
    11:3–7, Beloved sick not to death; stayed two days (4:40)
        11:8–10, The light of the world (8:12; 1:4)
    11:11–15, Beloved sleeps; dead; resurrection
11:16–17, Thomas: "Let us die with him"; Lazarus four days in the tomb

11:18–37, The Resurrection and the Life

This section begins and ends with references to "the Jews" who console Martha and Mary over the death of Lazarus (11:18–19, 36–37). The second and second-to-last sections present Jesus' interaction first with Martha (11:20–24) then with Mary (11:28–35), in which each says the same thing to him (11:21, 32). This structure spotlights the words of Jesus in 11:25–26, "I am the resurrection and the life," and Martha's confession of him in 11:27 as "the Christ, the Son of God who comes into the world."

11:18–19, Bethany, the Jews, Martha, and Mary
    11:20–24, Martha met him: "If you had been here, my brother would not have died"
        11:25–26, I am the resurrection and the life
        11:27, You are the Christ, the Son of God, who comes into the world
    11:28–35, Mary, where Martha met him: "If you had been here, my brother would not have died"
11:36–37, The Jews; he opened the eyes of the blind, kept this man from dying

Consider the way that the words of Jesus, "I am the resurrection and the life" (11:25), develop and apply what has been said about life to this point in the Gospel. We have seen that one of the Gospel's opening statements is "in him was life" (1:4), and we have seen Jesus assert that the Father granted the Son to have "life in himself" (5:26). For Jesus to assert himself as "the resurrection and the life" develops the earlier statement in a "darkness-has-not-overcome-it" (1:5) way. The life that is in the Father and the Son will not be overcome by death but will rather resurrect from death. In resurrection, life triumphs over death. Not only does this develop what has been said about life, it applies these earlier statements to those who have died. That Jesus is the resurrection and the life means that rather than the clean realm of life being polluted and killed by the spread of death, the unclean realm of the dead will be overrun by life, renewed and purified as the clean realm of life conquers through its king.

Several unstated implications force themselves to the surface as we consider Jesus asserting himself as the resurrection and the life. For death to be overcome, the cause of death, sin, must be defeated (cf. 1:29). For the formerly dead to be made clean to inhabit the realm of life, they must not only be given life, as though born anew, they must be cleansed from defilement, as though washed with water (cf. 3:3–8).

11:38–44, The Dead Hears the Voice of the Son of God

We saw unparalleled revelation about the relations between the Father and the Son in John 5:19–30, and now at the raising of Lazarus we see an unparalleled prayer from the Son to the Father at the center of this unit in 11:41–42. Surrounding that removal of the stone and prayer are words of Jesus promising the glory of God in 11:40 and delivering it by recalling Lazarus to life in 11:43. In the next ring out are references to the dead man in 11:39b and 11:44a, with the removal of the stone at the beginning in 11:38–39a and the removal of the grave clothes in 11:44b.

11:38–39a, Take away the stone
11:39b, Sister of the dead man: "Four days!"
11:40, If you believe, you will see the glory of God
11:41a, They took away the stone
11:41b–42, Jesus prays
11:43, Lazarus, come forth!
11:44a, The dead man came out
11:44b, Loose him and let him go

The connections between John 5 and 11 reinforce the notion that the healing of the lame man at the Pool of Bethesda portends the full restoration of resurrection, of which Jesus speaks in John 5, which he performs in John 11. Literary structure carries the message of fulfillment: The healing of the sick and raising up of the lame point beyond themselves to the liberation of creation from its bondage to corruption. That is to say, if Jesus can remove the weakness from the lame man's body, he can banish death from that of Lazarus. And he can do both because he has life in himself (5:26), and that life in himself is developed and applied in his identification of himself as the resurrection and the life (11:25).

The Old Testament looks forward to death being overcome, to the dead being raised and cleansed and renewed to dwell in the presence of God; which is to say, the Old Testament looks forward to Jesus.

New and Better Moses: John 6 and 10

The scope of this project does not afford space to go into the same level of detail for each section of John's Gospel. We will therefore summarize the points of contact between John 6 and 10 with an eye to how their standing across from each other in the book's literary structure makes the two chapters mutually interpretive. I will also put my proposals for the chiastic structures of these passages as excurses in this chapter. I would encourage readers to work carefully through the passages, preferably in Greek, examining the parallel phrases and ideas that stand across from one another in these chiastic structures. Patient study yields deepening insight.

The first and most obvious connection between John 6 and 10 has to do with the way that the new Moses is the good shepherd. Moses famously shepherded Israel through the wilderness to the land of promise, and under the ministry of Moses the Lord fed his people manna from heaven. After Jesus feeds the five thousand, the people recognize him as the Deuteronomy 18:15 prophet like Moses (John 6:14). In the same way that Moses ascended Mount Sinai alone, Jesus withdrew to a mountain by himself (6:15), and just as Moses led the people across the Red Sea, Jesus walked on water and brought his followers to dry land (6:16–21). By positioning John 10 across from John 6, John joins the prophesied good shepherd (Ezek. 34) to the prophesied new Moses, and he presents Jesus as the fulfillment of this expectation.

In John 6:35 Jesus identifies himself as the bread of life, and in 6:33 he had spoken of the bread of life coming down from heaven and giving life for the world. When Jesus speaks in John 10:15–18 of laying down his life for the sheep, readers of John's Gospel are helped to know what Jesus meant in John 6 when he spoke of the necessity of eating his flesh and drinking his blood (6:52–59). Jesus anticipates the way he will institute the Lord's Supper as a commemoration of his death and resurrection (see esp. 6:11, 23, and cf. Luke 22:14–23 and 1 Cor. 11:23–26) on the night he was betrayed, when he laid down his life for the sheep (John 10:15–18).

Finally, in John 6:45 John presents Jesus claiming that he brings the fulfillment of Isaiah 54:13. Those words in Isaiah had in fact extended what God promised to do for Moses to all God's people. When God called Moses at the burning bush, in the process of overcoming Moses' objections, the Lord promised, "I will be with your mouth and teach you what you shall speak" (Exod. 4:12 ESV). Isaiah prophesied of a time when all God's people would have the same experience: "All your children shall be taught by the Lord" (Isa. 54:13 ESV). And in John 6:45 Jesus claims that the realization of that new covenant blessing comes as those who have learned from the Father come to him: "It is written in the Prophets, 'And they will all be taught by God'" (ESV). This theme finds its echo in John 10 as Jesus declares that his sheep know his voice (10:3, 14, 27, 29).

EXCURSUS: PROPOSED CHIASTIC STRUCTURES FOR JOHN 6 AND 10

John 6:1–71, I Am the Bread of Life

6:1–17a, Jesus Feeds the Five Thousand
  6:17b–22, Jesus, the I Am, Walks on Water
    6:23–29, Work for Food that Remains to Life by Believing Jesus
      6:30–51, The Bread of Life to Whom Those Taught of God Come
    6:52–59, The Life-Giving Flesh and Blood of Jesus: True Food and Drink
  6:60–66, The Spirit and Life-Giving Words of Jesus
6:67–71, You Have the Words of Eternal Life, You Are the Holy One of God

6:1–17a, Jesus Feeds the Five Thousand

6:1–6, Across the sea, they saw the signs, Jesus went up on the mountain
  6:7, Two hundred denarii worth not enough for each to have a little
    6:8–9, What are five loaves and two fish for so many?
      6:10, Jesus had the five thousand men sit down
    6:11, Jesus took the loaves, gave thanks, and distributed

6:12–13, They ate their fill, had twelve baskets of leftovers

6:14–17a, They saw the sign, Jesus withdrew again to the mountain, across the sea

6:17b–22, Jesus, the I Am, Walks on Water

6:17b–18, Dark, sea

6:19, They see Jesus walking on the water

6:20, He says to them: I Am. Do not fear

6:21, They take him in the boat and immediately arrive

6:22, Next day, across sea

6:23–29, Work for Food that Remains to Life by Believing Jesus

6:23, They ate the bread after the Lord had given thanks

6:24–25, Rabbi, how did you come here?

6:26–27, Work not for the food that perishes but that remains

6:28, What must we do, to work the work of God?

6:29, This is the work of God: to believe him whom he sent

6:30–51, The Bread of Life to Whom Those Taught of God Come

6:30–34, Our fathers ate the manna in the desert

6:35, I Am the bread of life . . . the one who believes

6:36–38, Seeing, not believing, given by the Father, came down

6:39–40, I will raise him up on the last day

6:41, The Jews grumbled

6:42, Is this not? Do we not? How can he say?

6:43, Jesus told them not to grumble

6:44, I will raise him up on the last day

6:45–46, It is written, taught of God, from the Father, seeing

6:47–48, The one who believes . . . I Am the bread of life

6:49–51, Your fathers ate the manna in the desert

6:52–59, The Life-Giving Flesh and Blood of Jesus: True Food and Drink

6:52, A dispute among the Jews

6:53, Unless you eat and drink you have no life in you

6:54, He who eats my flesh and drinks my blood has life

6:55, My flesh is true food, my blood is true drink

6:56–57, He who eats my flesh and drinks my blood remains in me

6:58, The one who eats this bread will live to the age

6:59, In the synagogue at Capernaum

6:60–66, The Spirit and Life-Giving Words of Jesus

6:60, Many from the disciples: this is a hard word

6:61, Jesus, knowing in himself they were grumbling, said . . .

6:62, If you see the Son of Man ascending where he was before?

6:63, The Spirit gives life, Jesus' words are Spirit and life

6:64, Jesus knew who believed and who would betray

6:65, Jesus said: this is why I said no one can come unless . . .

6:66, Many from the disciples left and no longer followed

6:67–71, You Have the Words of Eternal Life, You Are the Holy One of God

6:67a, The twelve

6:67b, Do you want to go away?

6:68, Simon Peter answered: you have the words

6:69, We have believed and know

6:70–71a, Jesus answered: one of you is a devil (Judas)

6:71b, This one was about to betray him

6:71c, The twelve

John 10:1–42, The Good Shepherd

10:1–6, The Sheep Hear the Shepherd's Voice

10:7–10, I Am the Door for the Sheep

10:11–14, I Am the Good Shepherd

10:15–18, I Lay Down My Life for the Sheep

10:19–42, My Sheep Hear My Voice

John 10:1–6, The Sheep Hear the Shepherd's Voice

10:1, The one who does not enter by the door is a thief and a robber

10:2, The one who enters by the door is the shepherd of the sheep

10:3, To him the gatekeeper opens; the sheep hear his voice

10:4, The sheep follow him

10:5, They will not follow but flee from the stranger

10:6, This similarity he spoke to them

10:7–10, I Am the Door for the Sheep

10:7, Truly, truly, I am the door of the sheep

10:8, All who came before me were thieves and robbers

10:9, I am the door; if anyone enters through me he will be saved

10:10, The thief comes to steal, kill, and destroy, I came to give abundant life

10:11–14, I Am the Good Shepherd

10:11, I am the good shepherd

10:12a, The hired hand

10:12b, He sees the wolf coming

10:12c, And he leaves the sheep and flees

10:12d, And the wolf snatches and scatters

10:13, Because he is a hired hand

10:14, I am the good shepherd

10:15–18, I Lay Down My Life for the Sheep

10:15a, Just as the Father knows me and I know the Father

10:15b, And I lay down my life for the sheep

10:16, I have other sheep not of this fold

10:17, On account of this the Father loves me: because I lay down my life, that I may take it up again

10:18a, No one takes my life from me, but I lay it down of myself

10:18b, I have authority to lay it down and authority to take it up again

10:18c, This command I received from my Father

10:19–42, My Sheep Hear My Voice

10:19–22, Many were saying; others were saying

10:23, Jesus was walking in the temple in the colonnade of Solomon

10:24–26, Jesus answered them, the works that I do in my Father's name, you do not believe

10:27–30, My sheep hear my voice; I give them eternal life; the Father who gave them to me; I and the Father are one

10:31–38, Jesus answered them, good works from the Father, believe

10:39, They were seeking to seize him, but he went out from their hand

10:40–42, Many came to him and were saying; many believed

Your Eyes Shall See Your Teacher: John 7 and 9

A number of verbal points of contact link John 7 and 9 with each other. We will summarize this evidence, then reflect on how the disputes about Jesus in these two chapters mutually inform each other. Following this discussion is another excursus with the proposed literary structures for the two chapters.

Both John 7 and John 9 contain reports of various things said by various people. Consider John 7:11–12 side by side with 9:8–9.

John 7:11–12 (ESV)	John 9:8–9 (ESV)
[11] The Jews were looking for him at the feast, and saying, "Where is he?" [12] And there was much muttering about him among the people. While some said, "He is a good man," others said, "No, he is leading the people astray."	[8] The neighbors and those who had seen him before as a beggar were saying, "Is this not the man who used to sit and beg?" [9] Some said, "It is he." Others said, "No, but he is like him." He kept saying, "I am the man."

Another such instance comes in the wording of 7:25–26, where they ask of Jesus in 7:25, "Is this not . . . ?" And then answer in 7:26, "This is." The very same phrases, "Is this not?" and "This is" can be found in 9:8–9. Similar wording to the "others were saying" language in 7:12 can be found—the exact same phrase, in fact—in 9:16.

In 7:27 they speak of where the Christ comes from (πόθεν ἐστίν), and the very same phrase appears in the discussion of where Jesus comes from in 9:29–30. (The only other instance of this phrase in all the New Testament is in reference to where the wine came from in John 2:9.)

The blind man humorously asks the opponents of Jesus in John 9:27, "Do you also want to become his disciples?" (ESV). And this reminds readers of the way that the opponents fired at Nicodemus in 7:52, "Are you from Galilee too?" (ESV).

It is interesting to observe that Moses features prominently in the discussion in both John 7:19–23 and John 9:28–29. With Abraham featuring prominently in John 8:33–58, we can observe that there is a Moses-Abraham-Moses A-B-A′ movement in John 7, 8, and 9.

The disputes in John 7 and 9 frame the central conflict in John 5–11, the clash in John 8. There Jesus will come right out and tell his opponents that if they do not believe that he is the I Am, they will die in their sins (8:24). He will also tell them that they are of their father the devil (8:44).

EXCURSUS: PROPOSED CHIASTIC STRUCTURES FOR JOHN 7 AND 9

John 7:1–52, If Anyone Is Thirsty, Let Him Come to Me and Drink

> 7:1–9, (Galilee) Jews Seeking to Kill, Brothers Challenge Him, Feast of Booths
>
> > 7:10–29, Jesus, Whom They Sought to Kill, Spoke Openly at the Feast

7:30–44, Desire to Arrest, No Hands Laid, Seek Not Find, Thirst-Quenching Spirit

7:45–52, Have Any Rulers or Pharisees Believed? (Galilee)

7:1–9, (Galilee) Jews Seeking to Kill, Brothers Challenge Him, Feast of Booths

7:1a, In Galilee

7:1b–2, Jews seeking to kill him, Feast of Booths

7:3, His brothers said to him

7:4, For no one

7:5, For not even

7:6, Jesus said to them

7:7–8, World hates me, you go to the Feast

7:9, In Galilee

7:10–29, Jesus, Whom They Sought to Kill, Spoke Openly at the Feast

7:10–14, No one spoke openly of him

7:15–18, The Jews marveled

7:19, Why do you seek to kill me?

7:20, Who seeks to kill you?

7:21–24, I did one work and you all marvel

7:25–29, And behold, he speaks openly

7:30–44, Desire to Arrest, No Hands Laid, Seek Not Find, Thirst-Quenching Spirit

7:30, Pharisees sent officers to arrest him, no one laid a hand on him

7:31–32, From the crowd many believed, Christ, Pharisees opposed

7:33–36, You will seek me and not find me, and where I am you are not able to come

7:37–39, If anyone is thirsty let him come to me and drink; Jesus fulfills the water-giving rock by the Spirit

7:40–43, From the crowd, Prophet, Christ, some opposed, division

7:44, Some wanted to arrest him, no one laid hands on him

7:45–52, Have Any Rulers or Pharisees Believed? (Galilee)

7:45, Pharisees: why not arrested?

7:46, Officers: no one ever spoke like him

7:47, Pharisees: you have not also been deceived?

7:48, Have any of the rulers or Pharisees believed in him?

7:49, This crowd that does not know the law is accursed

7:50–51, Nicodemus: does our law condemn without hearing?

7:52, You are not also from Galilee?

John 9:1–41, Sight for the Man Born Blind

9:1–7, Blindness, sin, light of the world, healing

9:8–16, I am; where is he? This man is not from God. Sinner

9:17, He is a prophet

9:18, The Jews did not believe

9:19, How does he now see?

9:20, His parents answered

9:21, Ask him; he is of age

9:22, Confess Christ, out of synagogue

9:23–24, He is of age; ask him

9:25, He answered

9:26, How did he open your eyes?

9:27, I told you and you did not listen

9:28–29, We are disciples of Moses

9:30–34, Where he comes from, sinners, if he were not from God

9:35–41, Son of Man, worship, blindness, sin

The Life Was the Light of Men: John 8

Whereas there have been skirmishes in the buildup to John 8, when we come to this chapter we enter open conflict. In John's Gospel the Jews began persecuting Jesus at 5:16, seeking his death at 5:18. Prior to that there had been inquiries about the Baptist in 1:19–25, questions about Jesus' authority in 2:18, and then the conversation with Nicodemus in 3:1–21 followed by a discussion between some of the Baptist's disciples and a Jew in 3:25. Once we enter John 5–11, the hostility comes into the open at 5:16–18, but Jesus does a lot of unimpeded teaching through the rest of John 5 and all of John 6. In John 7 there is the initial avoidance of a public display (the hour has not come for a triumphal entry in 7:1–9), and though the crowds are surprised that Jesus speaks openly (7:25–26) and the officials are trying to arrest him (7:30), there are no direct confrontations with his opponents (7:32–52).

The initial clashes in places like 7:20 ("You have a demon!" [ESV]) anticipate the extended engagement in John 8. After the confrontation in John 8, which is the centerpoint of the chiasm that spans John 5–11, John 9 is like John 7 again, with Jesus quietly doing his thing as his opponents pursue a proxy-conflict with the man born blind and anyone saying Jesus is the Christ (9:13–23). For his own part, Jesus seems intent on avoiding another open dispute like the one in John 8, playing the part of David hiding from Saul, avoiding all-out war. Then the public teaching in John 10 matches the public teaching in John 6, before the raising of Lazarus forms the latch with the healing of the man at the Pool of Bethesda.

8:12–20, The Light of the World Renders True Attested Judgment from the Unknown

The confrontation in John 8 begins in the first section of the passage, 8:12–20, with Jesus declaring himself to be the light of the world (8:12),[5] and much as the darkness would like to, in the end it cannot overcome the light (8:20). Then follows a dispute about what kind of testimony counts for those seeking to do justice by rendering a true verdict. In second (8:13–14) and second-to-last (8:18–19) positions Jesus argues that he and the Father (whom they do not know) comprise the requisite two witnesses. In central position stands a passage in which Jesus indicts his opponents for judging according to the flesh (8:15), which stands across from the affirmation of the biblical standard demanding two witnesses (8:17), putting the testimony of Jesus and the Father dead center (8:16) as valid testimony resulting in a true verdict (judgment).

The chiastic structure of the passage looks like this:

> 8:12, Again then Jesus spoke: I am the light of the world
>
> > 8:13–14, You bear witness about yourself; even if I bear witness about myself; I know whence I came and where I go; you do not know

5. Notice the double brackets around John 7:53–8:11 in most translations. This is the publisher's way of alerting readers to the fact that this section is not original to the Gospel of John. It does not belong in the text, and I am convinced that John did not write this passage, nor did he intend it to interrupt the move from what is now enumerated 7:52 to 8:12. See further James M. Hamilton Jr., "John 7:53–8:11 Should Be in a Footnote, Not in the Text," *For His Renown* (blog), March 30, 2014, http://jimhamilton.info/2014/03/30/john-753-811-should-be-in-a-footnote-not-in-the-text/.

8:15, You judge according to the flesh

8:16, My judgment is true, the Father is with me

8:17, The law says the testimony of two men is true

8:18–19, I am the one who bears witness about myself; where is your Father? You know neither me nor my Father

8:20, These words he spoke; the darkness could not arrest him

8:21–30, I Am: What I Have Been Telling You from the Beginning

John then presents Jesus turning the dial on the audacity meter all the way up. In John 8:21–30, through the concentric circles of which we will move down to its center, Jesus begins by telling those opposed to him that they will die in their sins (8:21), a word of judgment through which many come to salvation by faith (8:30). While the Jews engage in crazy-talk speculation that Jesus might commit suicide (8:22), Jesus affirms that the Father has not abandoned him but is with him (8:29). And then Jesus contrasts himself with his opponents, telling them that while they are from below, from this world, he is from above, not of this world (8:23), in that he speaks and acts not on his own initiative but only as the Father taught him (8:28b). And then framing the central statements of this unit are two astonishingly bold "I Am" statements: In the first, Jesus tells his opponents that unless they believe he is the I Am, they will die in their sins (8:24); in the second, he tells them that when they have lifted up the Son of Man, they will know that he is the I Am (8:28a). In central position stands their direct question about who Jesus is, with its intriguingly worded reply in 8:25, accompanied by his assertion in 8:26 that the Father is true and that he, Jesus, accurately represents him.

The chiastic structure of John 8:21–30 falls out like this:

8:21, You will die in your sins; where I go you are not able to come

8:22, The Jews were saying, "Will he kill himself?"

8:23, He was saying to them, "You are from below; I am from above. You are of this world; I am not of this world."

8:24, If you do not believe that I Am, you will die in your sins

8:25, They were saying to him, "Who are you?"; Jesus said to them, "What I have been telling you from the beginning"

8:26–27, The one who sent me is true, and what I have heard from him, these things I speak to the world

8:28a, Jesus said to them, "When you have lifted up the Son of Man, then you will know that I Am"

8:28b, From myself I do nothing but as the Father taught me

8:29, The one who sent me is with me; he has not left me alone

8:30, While he was saying these things, many believed in him

8:31–47, Jesus and His Father, the Opponents and Theirs

If the Jewish opponents of Jesus didn't like him healing on the Sabbath (5:16–18) or telling them to eat his flesh and drink his blood (6:52), how will they respond to him telling them they will die in their sins (8:21), demanding that they recognize him as the I Am (8:24, 28), and claiming that he has the corner on the truth market (8:25–26)? With the conflict finally in the open, Jesus models how to engage the serpent and his seed: by not giving an inch. Ever since the garden, when the serpent used faux moral outrage to undermine Eve's trust in the Lord ("Has God really said?"—as though he cares), the serpent and his seed have been claiming the moral high ground, then using God's righteous standard to denounce God himself and those who belong to him. Jesus will have none of it.

In John 8:31–47 Jesus tells his opponents that they are seed of the serpent, and he is crystal clear on what distinguishes them from the seed of the woman (cf. Gen. 3:15; Rev. 12:1–17). Here again we will work through this passage by moving up its corresponding steps on either side to its central, pinnacle statements in the middle. Jesus begins (8:31–32) and ends (8:45–47) with the decisive point: his own word. Those who hear his word and abide in it are truly his disciples, they know the truth, and the truth liberates them (8:31–32). Those who are of God, the seed of the woman, hear God's words; the seed of the serpent do not (8:47). Thus, though Jesus speaks the truth, and though they cannot convict him of sin, the seed of the serpent do not believe him (8:45–46).

In response to his articulation of the dividing line in John 8:31–32, the opponents of Jesus protest that they are seed of Abraham and have never been enslaved in 8:33. In the corresponding statement near the end of the unit, Jesus will tell them in no uncertain terms what seed they are: "You are of your father the devil" (8:44 ESV). To address their mistaken notion that they are free, Jesus tells them in 8:34 that anyone who sins is a slave of sin, and in the corresponding statement in 8:43 he explains to them why they do not understand what he says: They are unable to hear his word. In 8:35–36 Jesus contrasts himself, the Son, with his opponents, the slaves—this implies his sinless freedom—and he asserts that those whom the Son frees experience true freedom. The corresponding statements in 8:41–42 find Jesus contrasting his Father with the father of his opponents, that slaver the devil. If God were their Father, Jesus explains in 8:42, they would love Jesus (cf. 1 John 3:9; 4:6, 7–12). This brings us to the statements that frame those at the center, and 8:37 and 8:40 deal with what it means to be seed of Abraham. Jesus acknowledges in 8:37 that his opponents physically descend from Abraham and claim to be his seed, but he points out to them that they seek to kill him because his word has no place in them. Complementing this statement in 8:40, Jesus repeats the idea that his opponents seek to kill him, a man who spoke to them the truth he heard from God, adding that Abraham did not try to kill his God.

In the central statements of this unit, Jesus asserts in John 8:38 that he speaks what he saw with his Father, and they do what they heard from theirs. In response, they insist that they are children of Abraham in 8:39, and Jesus tells them that if they were they would love him.

The chiastic structure of John 8:31–47 can be depicted thus:

> 8:31–32, Jesus said to the Jews who believed in him, "If you abide in my word; you will know the truth, and the truth will free you"
>
> > 8:33, They answered him, "We are seed of Abraham"
> >
> > > 8:34, Everyone who does sin is a slave to sin
> > >
> > > > 8:35–36, The slave does not abide in the house; the Son abides forever; if the Son frees you, you will be truly free
> > > >
> > > > > 8:37, I know that you are seed of Abraham; you seek to kill me because my word has no place in you
> > > > >
> > > > > > 8:38, I speak what I have seen with the Father; and you do what you heard from your father
> > > > > >
> > > > > > 8:39, Our father is Abraham! If you are children of Abraham, do the deeds of Abraham
> > > > >
> > > > > 8:40, You seek to kill me, a man who spoke to you the truth; this Abraham did not do

8:41–42, You do the works of your father; if God were your Father, you would love me

8:43, Why do you not know my speech? Because you are not able to hear my word

8:44, You are of your father the devil

8:45–47, Because I speak the truth, you do not believe in me; the one who is of God hears the words of God; you are not of God

It is hard to imagine more contested categories being discussed between Jesus and his opponents. In 8:12–20, he told his opponents that he was the true light, that he and his Father constituted two reliable witnesses, and that his judgment against them was true. He then proceeded in 8:21–30 to assert his identity with the Father, demanding that they recognize him as the I Am. His next move, in 8:31–47, was to explain why they refused to believe him: because they are seed of the serpent. He concludes in John 8:48–59 by telling them they do not know God.

8:48–59, You Have Not Known Him; I Know Him

God created this fabulous world, made humanity in his own image and likeness, gave Adam and Eve to each other, and turned them loose to thrive and flourish, to relish and rejoice. In that situation the ancient serpent had the temerity to insinuate that God was withholding good from Adam and Eve, and they took the bait.

That same liar who posed the poisonous question in the beginning now animates those who ask, "Are we not right in saying that you are a Samaritan and have a demon?" (John 8:48 ESV). These filthy lies are worthy of the one rightly called "a murderer from the beginning" and "the father of lies" (8:44 ESV). Jesus tells them, truly, that while he honors the Father, they dishonor him (8:49). Just as lies do not become true because they have been spoken, so those who would stone Jesus do not succeed by desiring their objective (8:59). This account opens with the seed of the serpent telling lies about Jesus (8:48–50) and closes with them wanting to murder him (8:59).

The Jews then object to Jesus saying that those who keep his word will not see death, asserting that even Abraham and the prophets died (8:51–52). In the corresponding statements they express incredulity that Jesus claims Abraham rejoiced over him, and Jesus says, "Before Abraham was, I Am" (8:57–58). In the ring inside that one, the Jews ask Jesus if he is greater than Abraham (8:53), and he tells them Abraham rejoiced to see his day (8:56). At the center of this chiastic structure Jesus asserts that the Father, whom they claim as God, glorifies him (8:54), telling them that they do not know God but he, Jesus, knows him and keeps his word.

The chiastic structure of John 8:48–59 is as follows:

> 8:48–50, You are a Samaritan and have a demon; I do not have a demon but honor my Father, while you dishonor me
>
>> 8:51–52, If anyone keeps my word, he will never see death; now we know that you have a demon; Abraham died along with the prophets
>>
>>> 8:53, Are you greater than our father Abraham, who died? And the prophets died
>>>
>>>> 8:54, The Father, whom you claim as your God, glorifies me
>>>>
>>>> 8:55, You have not known him; I know him, and his word I keep
>>>
>>> 8:56, Abraham your father rejoiced to see my day
>>
>> 8:57–58, You do not yet have fifty years and you have seen Abraham? Before Abraham was I Am
>
> 8:59, They picked up stones to stone him, but Jesus hid himself and went out from the temple

8:12–59, The Climactic Conflict of John 5–11

We can summarize the flow of thought in John 8:12–59 with the following chiastic structure built from the individual chiasms:

> 8:12–20, The light of the world renders true attested judgment from the unknown
>
> > 8:21–30, I Am; what I have been telling you from the beginning
> >
> > 8:31–47, Jesus and his Father; the opponents and theirs
>
> 8:48–59, You have not known him; I know him

This literary structure places John 8 at the pinnacle of the pedimental structure of John 5–11, explaining why this most heated public confrontation is placed here rather than immediately prior to the arrest of Jesus. Throughout John 1–11, Jesus' hour (2:4; 7:30; 8:20) or time (7:8) has not come, but it arrives in John 12–17 (12:23, 27; 13:1, 31; 17:1).

John 5–11 has taken place in public, among the crowds, at a number of feasts. John 12–17, by contrast, will take place in private, with the disciples, at the final Passover.

Questions for Reflection and Discussion

1. John presents Jesus forcing the issue on his opponents: Are they with Jesus and God, or are they with the serpent and his seed? What does John show to be the decisive factor in the answer to that question? How does this relate to what John states as his purpose in writing the Gospel (see 20:31)?
2. Throughout John's narrative, the protagonist (Jesus) and his opponents (unbelieving Jewish religious leaders) seem totally believable and never caricatured. How does John accomplish this, and what enables him to do it?

Suggested Reading

Gregory of Nazianzus. *On God and Christ: The Five Theological Orations and Two Letters to Cledonius*. Translated by Frederick Williams and Lionel R. Wickham. Popular Patristics Series. Crestwood, NY: St. Vladimir's Seminary Press, 2002.

Hamilton, James M., Jr. "John." In *John–Acts*, by James M. Hamilton Jr. and Brian J. Vickers. ESV Expository Commentary 9, edited by Iain M. Duguid, James M. Hamilton Jr., and Jay Sklar. Wheaton: Crossway, 2019.

Hamilton, James M., Jr. "The Lord's Supper in Paul: An Identity-Forming Proclamation of the Gospel." In *The Lord's Supper: Remembering and Proclaiming Christ Until He Comes*, edited by Thomas R. Schreiner and Matthew R. Crawford. Nashville: B&H, 2010.

Hamilton, James M., Jr. "The Skull Crushing Seed of the Woman: Inner-Biblical Interpretation of Genesis 3:15." *The Southern Baptist Journal of Theology* 10, no. 2 (2006): 30–54.

6

THE HOUR HAS COME

In Private, with Disciples, at Passover in John 12–17

> A marvellous and mighty paradox has thus occurred,
> for the death which they thought to inflict on Him as
> dishonour and disgrace
> has become the glorious monument to death's defeat.
>
> —Athanasius, *On the Incarnation* §24[1]

The two large central sections of John's Gospel balance each other. In John 5–11, Jesus is in public, at feasts, among the crowds, and the hour has not come (e.g., 8:20). After the Gospel's central turning point discussed in chapter 2 above, the counterweight to John 5–11 comes in John 12–17, where Jesus is in private, at the final Passover, with his disciples, and the hour has come (12:23; 13:1; 17:1).

John's strategic arrangement of his material is brilliant. He has built chapters 12–17 as a chiastic structure, the components

1. Athanasius, *On the Incarnation: De Incarnatione Verbi Dei* (Crestwood, NY: St. Vladimir's Seminary Press, 1988), 54.

of which also comprise a wider chiasm spanning chapters 5–17. Understanding this chiastic structure puts us in position to summarize what John intends his audience to learn about Jesus in this section of his Gospel. Starting at its central unit and working out through the concentric rings, we can say that here John presents Jesus calling his followers to abide in him, the true vine (15:1–15). Immediately surrounding that central idea are sections on how the disciples are not to be troubled by Jesus' departure but to trust him and God (14:1–31), even as the world hates them as it has hated him (15:16–27). The abiding in Christ at the center (15:1–15) will enable them to trust (14:1) and remember that they follow a persecuted Savior (15:20). The next ring out has Jesus preparing his disciples for his departure by washing their feet (13:1–38) and teaching them the benefits of his departure to the cross (16:1–33). The outer rings of this unit present Jesus announcing that the hour has come, calling on the Father to glorify him, and speaking to his disciples about following him in life-giving death that results in unity among themselves and with him and his Father by the Spirit (12:20–50; 17:1–26).

The chiastic structure of John 12–17 can be depicted as follows:[2]

John 12:20–50, The hour has come for the Son of Man to be glorified

  John 13:1–38, Footwashing; Jesus prepares his disciples

    John 14:1–31, Let not your hearts be troubled

      John 15:1–15, I am the true vine

    John 15:16–27, If the world hates you

  John 16:1–33, Jesus prepares his disciples for his death and resurrection

John 17:1–26, The hour has come; glorify your Son that your Son may glorify you

2. I think this proposal improves upon that of Wayne Brouwer, *The Literary Development of John 13–17: A Chiastic Reading*, SBL Dissertation Series 182 (Atlanta: Society of Biblical Literature, 2000).

Whereas in John 1–11 the literary structure advanced John's message of how Jesus brings Old Testament fulfillment, in John 12–21 the focus shifts, and here again the literary structure is John's medium for the message, teaching that abiding in Christ and the Father through the Spirit produces conformity to Christ in his death and resurrection.

In the summary above we started at the center and worked out through the concentric circles. In the body of this chapter we will reverse that and start with the outer rings, working our way down to the central teaching on abiding in Christ. Having worked our way through John 12–17 in this fashion, we will conclude with reflections on what John intends from the way the constituent units of this section also appear to be intentionally aligned with the constituent units of John 5–11, resulting in a chiastic structure that spans the whole of John 5–17.

The Hour Has Come: John 12 and 17

John 12:20–50 and 17:1–26 are each chiastically structured, and the units of each seem to correspond to one another, as can be discerned from consideration of the two in side-by-side alignment as follows:

John 12:20–50	John 17:1–26
12:20–29, The hour has come; glory	17:1–10, The hour has come; glory
12:30–36, Signifying his death	17:11–15, His joy fulfilled in us
12:37–43, Isaiah 53:1 and 6:9–10	17:16–20, As you sent me, I send them
12:44–49, Not to judge but to save	17:21–26, That they might be one that the world might know

The alignment of the four points on each of these chiastic structures informs the four subsections that follow, so that this discussion seeks to follow the way that John has structured his own material.

A Grain of Wheat Death Like His

It is remarkable that in both these texts, John 12 and John 17, Jesus prays, and in both he prays the same thing: for the Father to glorify the Son (12:27–28; 17:1). As we have seen often to this point, the subsections of wider chiastic structures are themselves chiastically structured. Thus, John 12:20–29 and 17:1–10 comprise chiasms, and presenting these structures allows me to summarize the section and gives readers a reminder of their contents.

12:20–29, Except a Grain of Wheat Fall into the Ground and Die

12:20–22, The Greeks want to see Jesus
  12:23, The hour; glorify
    12:24, Except a grain of wheat die, bear fruit
      12:25, He who loves his life will lose it; the one who hates his life in this world will keep it
    12:26, My servants follow me
  12:27–28, The hour; glorify
12:29, The crowd; thunder; angel (Sinai)

This section's closing, in light of its opening, is intriguing: the law of Moses was given through an angelic intermediary (Acts 7:38; Gal. 3:19; Heb. 2:2), and on that occasion there was thunder, as Israel became a nation by entering into covenant with the Lord. Now the Greeks have come to Jesus (John 12:20–22), and like Moses, Jesus speaks and God answers (Exod. 19:19), prompting some to say it thundered and others to say an angel spoke (John 12:28–29). On the cusp of the making of the new covenant, by this scene John reminds his audience of the making of the old.

The chiastic structure of this passage brings out the relationship between the hour as the cross, the glorification for which Jesus prays being what will happen on the cross (12:23, 27–28), and the way that Jesus himself is the grain of wheat that will die and then bear fruit (12:24).[3] What Jesus then goes on to say in 12:25–26 clearly indicates that he expects his disciples to, in the language found elsewhere, take up their cross and follow him (e.g., Luke 9:23). Not that they will literally be crucified, but that like him they will lay down their lives for the spiritual benefit of others.

17:1–10, Glorify the Son That the Son Might Glorify You

17:1, Glorify the Son that the Son might glorify you
- 17:2, That he might give eternal life to all you gave him
  - 17:3, Eternal life is knowing the true God and the sent Christ
    - 17:4, I glorified you on earth by completing the work
      - 17:5, Glorify me, Father, with the eternal glory
      - 17:6a, I manifested your name
    - 17:6b–7, To those you gave me from the world
  - 17:8, The words you gave to me I gave to them
- 17:9–10a, I ask for those you gave me not the world

17:10b, I am glorified in them

When we consider John 17:1–10 alongside John 12:20–29, the idea that the cross is where Jesus will be glorified is reinforced (17:1–2), but we also have Jesus speaking of how he has completed the work the Father gave him (17:4) and moving on to address the way he

3. Thomas Sculthorpe has suggested to me (private conversation) that from what Moses says about seed giving life and bearing fruit in Gen. 1:11–12, 29, when the same term appears in Gen. 3:15, the way the seed dies to give life and bear fruit could be suggested. If it is correct that the reason men are made unclean by the emission of seed in Lev. 15:16 is that life fluids have left the body and are regarded in some sense as no longer alive, uncleanness then resulting from contact with death, then a dying and rising conception also attaches to man's seed when it "falls into the ground" of his wife, dead seed giving new life in the womb.

will be glorified in those whom the Father gave him (17:6–10). It seems apparent from the juxtaposition of the statements here and in intervening chapters that Jesus will be glorified as his disciples love one another as he has loved them. In other words, as his disciples lay down their lives for their friends in the way he laid down his life for them, just as the Son thereby glorified the Father, so the disciples thereby glorify the Son.

The grain of wheat falls into the ground and dies, and the fruit of self-sacrificial love sprouts up from the dead seed to blossom for God's glory. As the disciples love others this way, they in turn will love as they have been loved. If that first grain of wheat, Jesus, dies, he indeed brings forth much fruit.

The Joy Set Before Him

The central statement in John 12:30–36 comes in 12:33, where John explains, "Now he was saying these things signifying what kind of death he was about to die." The central statement in 17:11–15 stands at verse 13, where Jesus says, "Now I come to you, and I say these things in the world, that they might have my joy fulfilled in themselves." The juxtaposition of these two statements brings out what Jesus demands and offers: He demands that his disciples take up the cross and follow him; he offers his own joy that results from self-giving love. The paradox here, that the joy of life is found in laying it down, is both the secret to Christlikeness and the transformative heart of self-denial. Once again displaying the chiastic structures will allow quick summary and review:

12:30–36, His Death

12:30, This voice not for me but you

  12:31, Now is the judgment of this world and its prince cast out

    12:32, If I am lifted up I will draw all men

      12:33, This he said signifying his death

12:34, How can you say the Son of Man must be lifted up?

12:35–36a, While you have the light walk in it

12:36b, Jesus said these things, went away, and was hidden

17:11–15, That They Might Have My Joy

17:11, Keep them in your name that they might be one

17:12, I kept those you gave me that the Scripture might be fulfilled

17:13, That they might have my joy fulfilled

17:14, I gave them your word

17:15, I do not ask that you take them out but keep them from

Putting these units side by side brings out the nature of the joy to which Jesus calls his followers. He wants them to have the joy of living out the love than which none is greater (15:13).

The Missions of the Son and His People

John interprets the mission of the Son as a fulfillment of what Isaiah saw in John 12:37–43. The people did not believe to fulfill Isaiah 53:1 and Isaiah 6:9–10, and Isaiah spoke those prophecies because he saw Christ's glory.

12:37–43, Isaiah 53:1 and 6:9–10

12:37, They did not believe him

12:38, To fulfill Isaiah 53:1

12:39–40, To fulfill Isaiah 6:9–10

12:41, Isaiah saw his glory

12:42, Many believed in him, but

Jesus was sent on a mission that would involve self-sacrificial love *because* he would be rejected. In 17:16–20 John presents

Jesus praying to the Father about the way he sends his followers on the same mission: to love as he loved, to be rejected as he was rejected. In this remarkable section of the prayer, the sanctification of the disciples by the word of God in 17:17 stands across from Jesus sanctifying himself that they might be sanctified in 17:19. Jesus sets himself apart and goes to the cross to make the disciples holy, and his word interprets and explains the cross, by which his followers know that the Father sent him to the cross, and by that word the disciples are sanctified.

17:16–20, As You Sent Me I Send Them

17:16, Like me they are not of this world

  17:17, Sanctify them in the truth, your word

    17:18, Just as you sent me I send them

  17:19, I sanctify myself that they might be sanctified

17:20, Not for these only but also those who believe through them

That the World Might Know

The chiastic structure of John 12:44–50 shows the centrality of the purpose for which Jesus came the first time—not to judge but to save:

12:44–50, Not to Judge but to Save

12:44–45, The one who sent me

  12:46–47a, Light; believe; words; judgment

    12:47b, I came not to judge the world but to save it

  12:48, Words; judgment

12:49–50, The one who sent me

In a similar way, the repeated reference to the world not knowing in John 17:21–26 (see 17:21, 23, 25) highlights the way that the followers of Jesus sharing in the unity of the Godhead is evangelistic.

Jesus came not to judge but to save, and as followers of Jesus love as Jesus loved, they experience union with the Godhead, which in turn produces unity among themselves, and by that love others know they are disciples of Jesus (cf. 13:35).

> **17:21–26, Union in Godhead and Church for the World to Know**
> 17:21, That they might be one, you in me and I in you, that the world might believe
> 17:22, The glory you gave me I gave them
> 17:23, I in them and you in me, that they might be perfectly one, that the world might know
> 17:24, That they might see my glory which you gave me
> 17:25–26, The world does not know; I made known to them that the love with which you loved me might be in them, and I in them

The juxtaposition of John 12:20–50 and 17:1–26 in the chiastic structure helps us discern what John intended to communicate by these passages. The Father will glorify Jesus through his sacrificial self-giving love on the cross, and disciples of Jesus are called to love as Jesus did. By doing this, they have the joy of Jesus, joy that results from loving that way, fulfilled in themselves. This, in fact, is the mission on which the Father sent the Son, and the Son in turn sends his followers the same way he was sent: united in love, enacting sacrificial self-giving, sanctified by the Word, not to judge the world but to save it.

Jesus Prepares His Disciples: John 13 and 16

In John 13 and 16 Jesus shepherds his disciples toward the fruit-bearing sacrificial self-giving that resolves in resurrection glory modeled and prayed for in John 12 and 17. In John 13 this shepherding takes the form of footwashing, followed by instruction on how the disciples should serve one another as Jesus has served them, concluding with predictions of betrayals and denials. In John 16, Jesus shepherds his disciples by explaining that his departure is necessary for the Spirit to come to them, the Spirit who will both convict them and lead them into truth. Their sorrow over his departure will turn to joy when he is raised from the dead, and they will enjoy new covenant blessings.

John 13 and 16 are each chiastically structured as follows:

13:1–38, Footwashing

13:1–11, The hour has come; Jesus washes the disciples' feet

  13:12–20, No servant is greater than his lord

  13:21–30, The traitor predicted and revealed

13:31–38, The hour has come; the new commandment

16:1–33, Jesus Prepares His Disciples for His Death and Resurrection

16:1–4, I have said these things to you; the hour is coming; I was with you

  16:5–7, I go to him who sent me

    16:8–11, The Spirit will convict of sin, righteousness, and judgment

      16:12–15, The Spirit will lead you into all truth

        16:16–19, Jesus' death and resurrection

      16:20–22, Sorrow of birth pangs; joy after childbirth

    16:23–26, In that day you will ask in my name

  16:27–30, I came from the Father and return to the Father

16:31–33, The hour is coming; I have said these things to you; the Father is with me

While there is not a one-to-one correspondence between these chiastic structures, there is a common movement of thought: The cleansing symbolized in the footwashing is not unlike the purifying power of the conviction of the Holy Spirit; the need to serve as Jesus served corresponds to being led into all truth by the Spirit; the revelation of the traitor results in sorrow like that spoken of with reference to the birth pangs; and the new commandment matches the new access to the Father the disciples will enjoy. In the discussion that follows we will briefly explore these matching ideas from John 13 and John 16.

Footwashing and the Conviction of the Spirit

Jesus both models service and symbolically cleanses his disciples when he washes their feet. The cleansing of the feet externally merely ratifies and symbolizes the cleansing of the heart internally by faith (13:10). John 13 opens with a contrast between Peter and Judas, as can be seen from consideration of the chiastic structure of John 13:1–11, and it likewise closes with a contrast between the same two men, with first Judas's betrayal (13:21–30) then Peter's denials (13:36–38) predicted.

13:1–11, Jesus Washes the Disciples' Feet

13:1, Jesus knowing
  13:2, Judas
    13:3–5, Washed feet (Jesus knowing)
  13:6–10, Peter
13:11, Jesus knew

John 13 and 16 correspond in their first sections in that the first part of 13 shows the believing disciples symbolically cleansed, and then the first part of 16 points to what must happen for the unbelieving world to be cleansed—they must experience the conviction of the Holy Spirit. A display of the first three chiastic units in John 16 will allow for a review of the statements there:

16:1–4, The Coming Hour of Persecution

16:1, I have said these things to keep you from falling away

16:2, The hour is coming when persecutors think they serve God

16:3, They do not know the Father or me

16:4a, When their hour comes remember I told you this

16:4b, I did not say these things from the beginning because I was with you

16:5–7, Better for You That I Go

16:5a, I go to him who sent me

16:5b, No one asks where I go

16:6, But because I said these things sorrow fills your heart

16:7a, But I tell you the truth: It is better for you that I go away

16:7b, For if I do not go, the Paraclete will not come to you

16:7c, But if I go, I will send him to you

16:8–11, He Will Convict the World

16:8a, He will convict the world

16:8b, Concerning sin and concerning righteousness and concerning judgment

16:9, Concerning sin, on the one hand, because they do not believe in me

16:10, Concerning righteousness, on the other hand, because I go to the Father and you will no longer see me

16:11a, Concerning judgment

16:11b, Because the ruler of this world has been judged

At the beginning (16:1–4) and end (16:31–33) of John 16 Jesus uses the same phrases as he warns of coming persecution: "these things I have spoken to you that," "an hour is coming," and he speaks of his presence with his disciples and the Father's presence with him. Because Jesus has spoken to them, they will not fall away (16:1) but have peace (16:33).

In the second (16:5–7) and second-to-last (16:27–30) units of John 16 he speaks of having come from and now returning to the Father. In response to their distress at his talk of leaving, in 16:7 he tells them it is better that he departs because if he does not do so the Spirit cannot come to them, but if he goes he will send the Spirit. In this case, the one sent of the Father (16:5) becomes the sender of the Spirit (16:7c).[4]

When the Spirit comes to the persecuted disciples, he will enable them to persevere in their sacrificial self-giving in imitation of Jesus, which will in turn be used to bring conviction of sin, righteousness, and judgment upon the unbelieving world (16:8–11). What Jesus does for the disciples by washing their feet is a symbolic sanctifying cleansing of them, that they might go into the world in the same way that Jesus sanctified himself and came into the world (17:19; cf. 10:36).

Jesus sanctified himself and came into the world to accomplish salvation. He then sanctifies his disciples and sends them into the world with the message of salvation. And he gives the Spirit to the disciples to convict the world, because the ruler of this world has been condemned (16:11b).

Christlikeness and the Leading of the Spirit into Truth

In the second part of John 13 (vv. 12–20), Jesus teaches his disciples that they must do for one another as he has done for them

4. I have argued elsewhere that the reason the Spirit cannot come to the disciples if Jesus does not go away is that the Spirit's coming to them will be the indwelling of the new temple of the Holy Spirit, the church. Jesus must go to the cross to fulfill the sacrificial system and the ministry of the temple if the Spirit is to take up residence in a new temple where no sacrifices are offered. See James M. Hamilton Jr., *God's Indwelling Presence: The Holy Spirit in the Old and New Testaments*, NAC Studies in Bible and Theology (Nashville: B&H, 2006).

in washing their feet (13:1–11). The chiastic structure of John 13:12–20 affords a swift review of the statements Jesus makes:

13:12–20, No Servant Is Greater than His Lord

13:12, When he had washed their feet

  13:13, I am teacher and Lord

    13:14, I washed your feet; wash one another's

      13:15, I gave you an example

        13:16, Truly, truly, no servant is greater than his Lord

      13:17, Blessed are you if you do these things

    13:18, He who ate my bread lifted his heel against me

  13:19, I tell you beforehand that you may know: I Am

13:20, Truly, truly, receive you; receive me

The central statements of this unit, that Jesus has given them the example of self-sacrificial service they must follow (13:15), that servants are not greater than their master (13:16), and that they are blessed if they do these things (13:17), constitute the heart of the truth into which the Spirit will lead the disciples (16:12–15) about Jesus' own death and resurrection (16:16–19).

16:12–15, The Spirit Will Lead You into All Truth

16:12, I still have much to say to you

  16:13a, When the Spirit of truth comes, he will lead you into all truth

    16:13b, For he will not speak from himself, but what he hears

  16:14, He will glorify me, because he will take what is mine and declare it to you

16:15, All that the Father has is mine

The Spirit will glorify Jesus (16:14) by teaching the disciples the meaning of Jesus' death. Just as Jesus did not speak from himself but what he heard (5:30), the Spirit speaks not from himself but what he hears (16:13b).

At this point in John's depiction, the disciples are clearly befuddled. They do not understand why Jesus departs, where he goes, or what he is talking about, as can be seen from the back-and-forth in John 16:16–19.

16:16–19, Jesus' Death and Resurrection

16:16, A little while and you will not see me, and again a little while and you will see me

  16:17a, They said to one another

    16:17b, What is this he says

      16:17c, Because I go to the Father

    16:18, What is this he says

  16:19a, He said to them

16:19b, A little while and you will not see me, and again a little while and you will see me

The disciples need the Spirit to lead them into all the truth about what Jesus accomplished on the cross (16:12–15), which they clearly do not understand (16:16–19), that they might follow Jesus' example of self-sacrificial service (13:12–20), that the world might be convicted of sin (16:8–11).

The Traitor, the Cross, and the Birth Pangs

In John 13:21–30 Jesus predicts Judas's betrayal, and in John 16:20–22 Jesus speaks of the sorrow his disciples will feel. In the chiastic structure of 13:21–30, the beloved disciple's question of who will betray, with the answer of Jesus, stands central (13:25–26). The inner frame has Peter motioning to the beloved disciple (13:24) and Satan entering Judas (13:27), another juxtaposition of Peter and Judas in John 13. The reclining disciples don't understand in 13:22–23 and 13:28–29, and Jesus' prediction (13:21) stands across from Judas doing the opposite of walking in the light, going out, "and it was night" (13:30).

13:21–30, The Traitor Predicted and Revealed

13:21, Jesus, troubled in spirit, predicts Judas's betrayal
- 13:22–23, Disciples don't understand; John reclining
  - 13:24, Peter motions to John
    - 13:25, John asks, "Who?"
    - 13:26, Jesus answers
  - 13:27, Satan enters Judas
- 13:28–29, Those reclining don't understand

13:30, Judas went out, and it was night

Corresponding to the distressing prediction in John 13:21–30 is the statement about the birth pang sorrow of the disciples in John 16:20–22. This sorrow, however, like birth pangs, gives way to joy, as Jesus hints at his resurrection.

16:20–22, Sorrow of Birth Pangs, Joy After Childbirth

16:20, You will weep, but the world will rejoice; your sorrow will turn to joy
- 16:21a, The woman giving birth has sorrow because her hour has come
  - 16:21b, When the child is born, she remembers not affliction
- 16:21c, For joy that a man has been born into the world

16:22, You have sorrow now; your hearts will rejoice

Neither the distress and sadness of betrayal nor the pains of childbirth are permanent. Both give way to new life.

The New Commandment, New Access, and New Peace

Both the end of John 13 and the end of John 16 look forward to what comes next. In the case of John 13 the prediction of Peter's looming denials accompanies the new commandment that comes with the inauguration of the new covenant (13:31–38). The glory of the Son of Man on the cross (13:31–32) brings a definitive end to the old covenant as the new is inaugurated, and with the making of the new covenant comes a new commandment (13:34; cf. Heb. 7:12).

13:31–38, Glory, New Commandment, Denials

13:31–32, Now is the Son of Man glorified

- 13:33, Where I go you are not able to come
  - 13:34, The new commandment
  - 13:35, They will know you are mine by your love
- 13:36, Where I go you are not able to follow

13:37–38, Prediction of Peter's denials

In John 16, Jesus first speaks of the new access his disciples will have to the Father in prayer as they come in his name (16:23–26), then he speaks of his return to the Father, perhaps beyond the cross at the ascension (16:27–30), and closes with words that repeat statements made in 16:1–4, Jesus assuring his disciples that in him they have peace because he has overcome the world (16:33).

16:23–26, In That Day You Will Ask in My Name

16:23, In that day you will ask . . . in my name

- 16:24a, Until now
  - 16:24b, Ask and you will receive, that your joy may be full
- 16:25, The hour is coming

16:26, In that day you will ask in my name

Because the old covenant is over, all who come to the Father come to him through Jesus, the great high priest, and prayer will now be offered in his name, granting his followers unprecedented access to God (16:23–26). In view of what Jesus says about joy elsewhere in John, it would seem that here the disciples pray for greater Christ-likeness, a prayer the Father will always answer, which will lead to them having the joy of Jesus himself in the exercise of sacrificial self-giving love (16:24).

16:27–30, I Came from the Father and Return to the Father

16:27, You have believed that I came from God
 16:28a, I came from the Father and came into the world
  16:28b, Again I leave the world and go to the Father
 16:29, Now you speak plainly!
16:30, We believe that you came from God

The disciples are confirmed in their faith in Jesus. This faith specifically affirms that Jesus was with the Father prior to coming into the world, that he came into the world from the Father, and that having completed the work the Father gave him to do (cf. 17:4), he leaves the world to return to the Father (16:27–30).

16:31–33, Reprise of 16:1–4: I Have Overcome the World

16:31, Do you now believe?
 16:32a, You will be scattered and leave me alone
  16:32b, I am not alone because the Father is with me
 16:33a, These things I have said that in me you may have peace
16:33b, In the world you will have trouble, but I have overcome the world

The closing words of John 16 point forward to the striking of the shepherd and the scattering of the sheep (16:32a), but even here the shepherd prepares them. As Jesus assures his disciples that even as they leave him alone he is not alone (16:32b), he sets them up to believe that in him they have peace (16:33a) because he has overcome the world (16:33b).

The death of Jesus inaugurates the new covenant. Members of the new covenant will obey the new commandment to love one another as Christ has loved them (13:34), and they will have new access to the Father in prayer as they come to him in the name of Jesus (16:23–26), experiencing the joy of Jesus himself (16:24), enjoying the peace he alone provides (16:33a) even as the nations continue to rage, causing the disciples tribulation in the world (16:33b).

Be Not Troubled, Even If the World Hates You: John 14 and 15:16–27

The inner frame around the central call to abide in Christ (15:1–15) consists of Jesus teaching his disciples not to let their hearts be troubled (14:1–31) even if the world hates them (15:16–27). The setting for the instruction in John 14 about not being troubled is the fact that at the end of John 13 Jesus has predicted that one of the disciples will betray him and that Peter will deny him.

In the face of that startling news, he tells them not to let their hearts be troubled at the beginning (14:1) and end (14:27) of the chapter. He also teaches that he is going away but will return for them at the beginning (14:2–3) and end (14:28). A sketch of the chiastic structure of John 14 will provide a summary of the chapter's contents:

14:1–31, Let Not Your Hearts Be Troubled

14:1–7, Do not let your hearts be troubled
- 14:8–11, The words I speak
  - 14:12–17, Love/keep
  - 14:18–21, Love/keep
- 14:22–26, The words I speak

14:27–31, Do not let your hearts be troubled

We can similarly quickly overview John 15:16–27 by means of its chiastic structure:

15:16–27, If the World Hates You

15:16, I chose you and appointed you to bear fruit

15:17, I command you these things for you to love one another

15:18, If the world hates you, know that it hated me first

15:19, If you were of the world; you are not of the world, so the world hates you

15:20, Remember the word; if they persecuted me; if they keep my word

15:21, These things they will do to you on account of my name, because they do not know the one who sent me

15:22–23, If I had not come and spoken to them; the one who hates me also hates my Father

15:24, If I had not done the works among them; they have hated me and the Father

15:25, To fulfill the word that is written in their law that they hated me without cause

15:26, The Paraclete will bear witness concerning me

15:27, And you will bear witness

In John 14 Jesus tells his disciples what will happen at the end: He will return for them. In John 15 he tells them what happened at the beginning: He chose them. We will consider these topics first, before moving to the power of the word of Christ in both sections, the coming persecution, and then the relationship between love and obedience, abiding and fruit bearing.

I Chose You and Will Come for You (Protology and Eschatology)

Jesus is the grain of wheat that dies to bear fruit (12:24), and he chose and appointed disciples who would do the same (15:16). Like him, they will lay down their lives for others because he chose them to bear the fruit of joyful self-giving love. The fact that he chose them for this means that he knows they will be persecuted, and it puts their suffering in the context of his purposes. This enables them to abide in him as they suffer, knowing both why they suffer and what it accomplishes.

The protology (understanding of first things) of election is accompanied by the eschatology (understanding of last things) of the Father's house, to which Jesus promises to bring his disciples when he returns for them (14:1–3). The unstated but implied imagery seems to envision the new heaven and new earth as the cosmic temple that Jesus goes to prepare (14:2). Just as the purpose of the original cosmic temple of creation was for God to dwell with his image bearers, the purpose of redemption is for Jesus and his followers to be together: "I will come again and will take you to myself, that where I am you may be also" (14:3b ESV).

The Power of Christ's Word

The power of the word of Jesus can be seen in a number of statements in John 14. Perhaps most remarkably, in 14:10 Jesus asserts that the Father does his *works* through the *words* that Jesus speaks. Jesus also asserts in this verse that he does not speak "from himself," indicating the inseparability of what he says from the Father's will (cf. also 5:19, 30; 16:13). The Father does his *works* through the *words* Jesus speaks, and at the end of the chapter Jesus asserts that he does just as the Father has commanded (14:31). There is a progression here from the Father's commands to the Son's action and teaching to what the disciples will then do and say.

We see the progression just alluded to reflected in the words of John 14:15 and 14:21. Jesus asserts in 14:15 that those who love him will keep his commands. Then in 14:21 he reverses the order of these statements, saying that the one who has his commands and keeps them is the one who loves him. Given John's teaching elsewhere (e.g., 6:63; 1 John 4:19), we can say with confidence that Jesus' word of command awakens love for Jesus, and once that love for Jesus is awakened by the command, the command is kept.

Jesus develops this further in John 14:22–26, which has a chiastic structure as follows:

14:22–26, The Words I Speak

14:22, What has happened that you manifest yourself to us and not the world?

  14:23, If anyone loves me he will keep my words; and we will make our home with him

    14:24, The one who does not love me does not keep my words

  14:25, These things I have said to you remaining with you

14:26, The Paraclete, whom the Father will send in my name

Here the central statement in John 14:24 has to do with those who do not love Jesus not keeping his words, and the framing statements in 14:23 and 14:25 both treat the benefits the disciples receive from the words of Jesus. As Jesus asserts in John 6:63, "The words that I have spoken to you are spirit and life" (ESV).

In John 15:16–27, the central statement in the chiastic structure is the assertion in 15:21 that the persecutors will oppose the disciples because of the name of Jesus, because they do not know the one who sent him. The immediate frame around this central statement shows that the word of Christ is the dividing line between those who know God and those who do not. In 15:20, Jesus commands his disciples to remember his word, which will give them confidence as they are persecuted by interpreting the persecution for them. He also asserts that those who keep his word will keep theirs. Then in 15:22 Jesus says that the persecutors would not have sin had he not spoken to them.

If They Persecuted Me

In most of John 14 Jesus calms the hearts of his disciples at the news of betrayal, denial, and his own departure. Near the end of the chapter, however, he may anticipate the trouble they will have from the world, which he will address in 15:16–27, when he says that he does not give them peace as the world gives in 14:27, and when he says the ruler of this world is coming in 14:30.

That coming persecution Jesus addresses straightforwardly in 15:18, when he tells his disciples that when the world hates them, they are to remember that it hated him first. This statement stands across from 15:25 in the chiastic structure of this section, where Jesus points to the fulfillment of Psalm 35:19 // 69:4, places where David spoke of being hated without cause. What was typified in David's experience is fulfilled in Jesus.

Matching "if" clauses stand across from each other in John 15:19 and 15:24. In 15:19, *if* the disciples were of the world, it would love them as its own. In 15:24, *if* Jesus had not done the works no one else had done among them, they would have no sin, but they have hated him. These statements frame the central remarks about the dividing line of the word discussed under the previous subheading ("The Power of Christ's Word").

Love and Obedience, Abiding and Fruit Bearing

The power of Christ's word not only divides those who love Jesus from those who do not, and it not only gives life to those who need to be born again: The power of Christ's word sparks love for Christ in his people, informing and empowering their obedience, drawing them so that they abide in him, communicating his presence to them, causing them to bear fruit. This theme receives direct treatment in John 15:1–15, but it is also anticipated in places like John 14:21, "The one who has my commandments and keeps them, he is the one who loves me. And the one who loves me will be loved by my Father, and I will love him and manifest myself to him." These statements do not indicate that when people love God they prompt God to love them (see esp. 1 John 4:19). Rather, these statements show the transformative power of the love of God communicated by the word of Christ. As Jesus speaks, love for God is produced by his command, as if he said: "Let there be love!" And God delights in the resulting love for God in the human heart. The human who has and keeps Christ's command is being conformed to God's own character, which God loves, in which he delights.

We see the same dynamic in John 14:23, "Jesus answered and said to him, 'If anyone loves me my word he will keep, and my Father will love him; and to him we will come, and our home with him we will make.'" The term rendered "home" in John 14:23 is the same term for "room" (ESV) in 14:2 ("In my Father's house are many *rooms*"). God is not prompted to love people when they love him (1 John 4:9–10). God loved the world by sending his Son (John 3:16), and those who received him were born of God (1:12–13). God gave Jesus the people who believe out of the world (6:37, 39, 44; 17:6–12). Those people, however, must abide in the words of Jesus if they are truly his disciples (8:31). They must have and keep the commands of Jesus (14:21), in which God will delight, to which he will respond with love (14:21, 23). These people will enjoy the abiding presence of God with them in Christ by the Spirit (14:23).

Because Jesus has chosen these people (15:16a), they will bear abiding fruit (15:16b)—because Jesus will send to them the Paraclete, who will bear witness to Jesus (15:26), prompting the people of Jesus also to bear witness to him (15:27).

Abide in Me: John 15:1–15

Repeated words and phrases signal the units of John 15:1–15 as well as their structure. As a whole the first half of John 15 falls out as follows:

15:1–15, I Am the True Vine
15:1–5a, I am the vine
  15:5b–8, The one who remains in me bears fruit
  15:9–12, Keep my commands and remain in my love
15:13–15, No greater love: to lay down one's life for friends

The natural divisions in the text will structure this discussion.

The True Vine

When Peter objected to Jesus washing his feet, Jesus explained that the one unwashed by him had no part with him. Peter then asked to be completely washed, and Jesus responded that the one who has bathed needs only his feet washed, and he said the words, "And you are clean" (13:10). That same language appears in John 15:3, where Jesus tells his disciples that they are already clean, in this context referring to having been pruned, because of the word he has spoken to them. That statement about the word having cleansed/pruned the people of Jesus is complemented by his command that they remain in him in 15:4, communicating the central ideas of John 15:1–5. Statements about fruit bearing form the inner frame, and then Jesus' assertions that he is the vine form the outer bracket around this unit of thought.

15:1–5a, I Am the Vine
15:1, I am the true vine
  15:2, Every branch not bearing fruit; bearing fruit he prunes
    15:3, You are already pruned because of the word I have spoken to you

15:4a, Remain in me, and I in you

15:4b, Just as the branch is not able to bear fruit by itself, so also you

15:5, I am the vine; you are the branches

This passage vividly illustrates what it is like for the disciples of Jesus to abide in him by means of constant meditation on the word. In the same way that Psalm 1 spoke of the blessed man being like a tree with roots near a stream, the water from the stream nourishing the tree the way the word nourishes the soul of the believer, so also John 15 speaks of Christ as the vine and his followers as branches, the word of Christ nourishing believers like life-giving nutrients that come to the branches from the vine.

Abiding in Christ

The outer statements in John 15:5b–8 speak of fruit bearing, and they enclose two "if" statements. Here again the emphasis is on remaining in Christ by night and day meditation on his word.

15:5b–8, The One Who Remains in Me Bears Fruit

15:5b, The one who remains in me and I in him, this one bears fruit

15:6, If someone does not remain in me

15:7, If you remain in me and my words remain in you

15:8, In this is my Father glorified, that you bear much fruit

From the surrounding context we can say that the word of Christ will cause the disciples, like grains of wheat, to fall into the ground and die. As they abide in Christ by meditating on the word, they will experience new life, and their self-sacrificial love for others will itself be fruit and will also bring about fruit in others. This process glorifies the Father as his own character is reflected back to him by image bearers growing in Christlikeness.

Obedience and Love

The progression from Father to Son, Son to disciples is on full display in John 15:9–12. The outer *inclusio* states first the Father's love for the Son and the Son's love for the disciples in 15:9a, and this is complemented in 15:12 by the Son's call for the disciples to love one another as he has loved them. In second and second-to-last positions Jesus calls his disciples to keep his commandments and remain in his love in 15:9b–10a, matching this with the explanation that this will make them have his joy, making their joy complete in 15:11. The central statement in this section stands in 15:10b, where Jesus holds himself out to the disciples as their example: They should do as he has done: he has kept his Father's commands, thereby remaining in the Father's love.

The chiastic structure of John 15:9–12 can be depicted as follows:

15:9–12, Keep My Commandments and Remain in My Love

15:9a, Just as the Father loved me, I also loved you

  15:9b–10a, If you keep my commandments you will remain in my love

    15:10b, Just as I have kept my Father's commandments and remain in his love

  15:11, These things I have spoken that my joy may be in you and yours complete

15:12, This is my commandment: Love one another as I have loved you

No Greater Love

The love to which Christ calls his people is the love he himself shows: that of laying down his life for his friends. This can be seen in the chiastic structure of John 15:13–15.

15:13–15, No Greater Love: To Lay Down One's Life for Friends

15:13, Greater love has no one than this: that someone lay down his life for his friends

    15:14, You are my friends if you do what I command

        15:15a, I no longer call you servants

        15:15b, because the servant does not know what his master does

    15:15b, I have called you friends

15:15c, Everything I heard from my Father I made known to you

The Father has loved Jesus, and Jesus does what the Father commands (15:15c), which is show the love than which none is greater (15:13). In the inner frame Jesus calls his disciples friends (15:14, 15b), and in the central statements he asserts that they are no longer servants (15:15a) and why (15:15b).

The Broader Message of John 5–17

John has brilliantly structured his presentation so that not only are John 5–11 and 12–17 chiasms unto themselves, together the whole of John 5–17 comprises a wide-angle chiasm through the book's central section.[5] By means of this arrangement, John presents Jesus calling his followers to abide in him, the good shepherd, the light of the world, through persecution to union with God and one another and resurrection glory.

5 and 17, Resurrection glory

    6 and 16, Jesus shepherds his people

        7 and 15:16–27, Controversy

            8 and 15:1–15, Following the light; abiding in Christ

5. See also the layout of this chiasm in Table 2.1 in chap. 2 above.

9 and 14, Controversy
10 and 13, Jesus shepherds his people
11 and 12:20–50, Resurrection glory

The healing of the lame man at the Pool of Bethesda in John 5 enacts fulfillment of the Sabbath and anticipates resurrection from the dead. It puts on display the glory Christ had with the Father before the foundation of the world, for which Jesus prays in John 17. Standing across from John 5 and 17 on the outer edges are John 11 and 12:20–50 on the inner edges, where Lazarus is raised from the dead, and where Jesus is the grain of wheat that falls into the ground and dies to bear much fruit.

John presents Jesus as the fulfillment of Moses, bread from heaven for those in the wilderness in John 6. That passage stands across from the teaching by which Jesus shepherds his disciples in John 16, teaching that imparts the Spirit, which Moses wished all God's people would have. The shepherding in John 6 and 16 is matched by the shepherding in John 10, where Jesus names himself the good shepherd, and John 13, where the shepherd serves his sheep by washing their feet.

There is controversy over whether Jesus will go to the feast in John 7, and those disputes anticipate the hatred of the world in John 15:16–17. The disputes in John 7 are matched by those in John 9, and the persecution in the latter half of John 15 is complemented by the distress of betrayal and denial in John 14.

At the center stands the light of the world in John 8, in whom his disciples must remain in John 15:1–15. John seems to signal that these passages stand across from each other by presenting Jesus saying in John 8:31, "If you abide in my word, you are truly my disciples" (ESV). That key concept informs the whole of John 15:1–15, as can be seen in John 15:7, where abiding in Jesus is having his words abide in you.

Questions for Reflection and Discussion

1. What does it look like for someone to abide in Christ? Would you describe yourself that way? What do you need to stop doing and start doing to be someone who abides in him?
2. In John 5–11 Jesus speaks in public, and in 12–17 he speaks in private. What stands out to you as prominent contrasts in the way Jesus speaks in these two blocks of material?

Suggested Reading

Cyril of Alexandria. *On the Unity of Christ*. Translated by John Anthony McGuckin. Crestwood, NY: St. Vladimir's Seminary Press, 1995.

Davis, Andrew M. *How to Memorize Scripture for Life: From One Verse to Entire Books*. Wheaton: Crossway, 2024.

Sculthorpe, Thomas John. "He Makes Her Desert Like the Garden of YHWH: A Typological Understanding of the Birth of Isaac as Resurrection from Death." PhD diss., The Southern Baptist Theological Seminary, 2024.

7

FROM GARDEN TO GARDEN

Jesus Arrested, Crucified, and Raised in John 18:1–20:18

> He dies, but he vivifies and by death destroys death.
> He is buried, yet he rises again.
>
> —Gregory of Nazianzus, *Oration* 29.20[1]

John 18:1–20:18 begins in a garden and ends in a garden, and its constituent parts form a chiastic structure. It thus stands as the complement to John 2–4, which began in Cana and ended in Cana, and whose constituent parts likewise form a chiastic structure. This chapter has two objectives: first, to highlight the correspondences between the units that make up the chiastic structure of John 18:1–20:18 and suggest biblical theological

1. Gregory of Nazianzus, *On God and Christ: Five Theological Orations and Two Letters to Cledonius*, trans. Frederick Williams and Lionel R. Wickham, Popular Patristics Series (Crestwood, NY: St. Vladimir's Seminary Press, 2002), 88.

conclusions that can be drawn from the literary structure; and second, to do the same with the corresponding sections in the wider chiastic structure of the whole Gospel, chapters 2–4 and 18–20.

The Chiastic Structure of 18:1–20:18

The first and last units of this section involve seeking Jesus in a garden. In the second and second to last, Peter and the other disciple travel together, the other getting there first, then both entering. In the third the Jews ask for Jesus' death, and in third to last he is dead. Fourth and fourth to last treat his trial before Pilate and the fulfillment of Scripture, and in the central section Christ is crucified. The chiastic structure can be depicted as follows:

18:1–11, Jesus arrested in a garden
  18:12–28, Peter and the other disciple follow Jesus
    18:29–40, The Jews ask for Jesus' death
      19:1–8, 8–13, Behold the man, Pilate sought to release
        19:14–22, The crucified king of the Jews
      19:23–30, Scripture fulfilled; it is finished
    19:31–42, Jesus dead
  20:1–11, Peter and the other disciple run to the tomb
20:12–18, Mary and Jesus in the garden

In this discussion we will work from the outer units in to the central.

18:1–11 and 20:12–18, Seeking Jesus in the Garden

Jesus enters the garden in John 18:1, and he is buried in a garden in 19:41. The only other reference to the garden is in 18:26. In 18:4 Jesus asks Judas and those with him, "Whom do you seek?" (ESV). In 20:15 Jesus poses the very same question to Mary Magdalene. In addition to the fact that Jesus is sought in a garden in both 18:1–11 and 20:12–18, there are also the supernatural manifestations in both accounts. Jesus says "I Am" to his arresters in 18:5, causing them to draw back and fall to the ground in 18:6. Mary first sees two angels in the tomb in 20:12, before seeing the *risen* Jesus in 20:14–16, who tells her he is ascending to the Father in 20:17. In both of these episodes, the first and the last of this unit, Jesus tells a follower not to do something. After Peter cuts off the ear of the high priest's servant in John 18:10, Jesus tells him to put the sword away in 18:11. Similarly, he tells Mary not to cling to him in 20:17.

Adam and Eve transgressed in the garden at the beginning. At the moment when Jesus is going to overcome their failure, he is arrested in a garden, buried in a garden, and stands risen in a garden. When we consider the garden in biblical theological terms, it is like the Holy of Holies, with the broader region of Eden being like the holy place, and the dry lands corresponding to the camp of Israel. It is fascinating, then, that just as there were cherubim on either side of the ark of the covenant in the Holy of Holies, so when Mary looks into the tomb she sees angels on either side of the place where Jesus lay, as though that place is the mercy seat on the ark of the covenant, overshadowed by the cherubim.

18:12–28 and 20:1–11, Peter and the Other Disciple

After the first and last episodes of this unit, in both the second and the second to last, Peter and the other disciple travel to where Jesus has been taken. In John 18:12–28 they follow Jesus to his interview with Annas, and in 20:1–11 they go to the tomb. In both cases, the other disciple arrives first, then Peter enters. In 18:15–16, because the other disciple is known to the high priest, he is able to enter the courtyard, then speak to the servant girl who grants access to Peter. In 20:4–5 the other disciple runs ahead of Peter, and on arrival at the tomb, looks in but does not enter. Then Peter arrives in 20:6 and enters the tomb, after which the other disciple does the same in 20:8.

In these narratives there is a contrast between Judas and Peter, and there is also an indication that not even betrayal can overcome the Lord Jesus. The contrast comes in the comparison arising from similarity: In 18:5 Judas is "standing with" those who have come to arrest Jesus; similarly, in 18:18 and 18:25, as Peter denies Jesus, he is "standing with" those warming themselves in the high priest's courtyard. We read no more of Judas in John's Gospel, but Peter's denial has not resulted in him abandoning the faith. Mary runs to Peter in 20:2, and Peter and the other disciple run to the tomb (20:3–4). The fact that the tomb is empty shows how not even treachery and betrayal overcome Jesus. Peter denied him, and they killed him, but nothing can keep him dead. Jesus is greater than Peter's failure.

18:29–40 and 19:31–42, Jesus' Death Sought and Accomplished

In both John 18:29–40 and 19:31–42 there are interactions with Pilate, there is fulfillment, there is information on Jesus' death, and there is bearing witness to the truth. We will work backward through this list.

As Jesus interacts with Pilate in John 18:29–40, he tells him in 18:37, "For this purpose I was born and for this purpose I have come into the world—to bear witness to the truth" (ESV). One of the themes of John's Gospel has to do with the disciples becoming Christlike. Jesus was in the bosom of the Father (1:18), and the beloved disciple reclines in Jesus' bosom (13:23). Jesus is a grain of wheat that must fall into the ground and die (12:24), and his disciples must do likewise (12:25–26). He has washed their feet, and they must wash one another's (13:14). They must love one another as he has loved them (15:12). And so also here: Jesus came into the world to bear witness to the truth (18:37), and in the corresponding section John asserts that he is bearing true witness (19:35).

As has already been noted above, in John 18:31 the Jews ask for Jesus' death, and then in the matching section in 19:33 we read that he is dead. What John has to say about fulfillment in these corresponding sections has far-reaching implications. In John 19:36 we read, "For these things took place that the Scripture might be fulfilled" (ESV), and then John references the instructions for the Passover lamb in Exodus 12:46. In John 18:32, by contrast, we read, "This was to fulfill the word that Jesus had spoken to show by what kind of death he was going to die" (ESV). The juxtaposition of these "fulfillment" statements strongly suggests that the words of Jesus in the Gospel of John are every bit as prophetic—which is to say, just as much the word of God—as the Scripture from Exodus fulfilled in 19:36. What John presents is tantamount to a claim that he has written Scripture.

Jesus and the Jews interact with Pilate in John 18:29–40, and the Jews interact with Pilate in 19:31–42. The back-and-forth in the two passages is enough in itself to prompt John's audience to see the similarities between them.

19:1–13 and 19:23–30, Trial and Fulfillment

In the central episode of this section, Jesus is crucified in John 19:14–22. Framing that central moment are 19:1–13 and 19:23–30. The term "took" seems to function significantly in these two units. John 19:1 opens with the statement, "Pilate took Jesus and flogged him" (ESV). Pilate's name then marks key movements of 19:1–13 at 19:1, 19:8, and 19:13. The corresponding section opens with the statement that the soldiers "took" the garments of Jesus at 19:23 and closes with the statement that Jesus "took" (ESV: "received") the sour wine in 19:30. Whereas Pilate and the soldiers "took" in ways that did violence, Jesus "took" what was appointed for him to fulfill Scripture, and the beloved disciple also "took" Jesus' mother into his care in 19:27, resulting in a thought-provoking contrast between the way Jesus and his followers "take" as compared with the way those who crucify "take."

The soldiers torture and mock Jesus in 19:2–3, and they crucify him and divide his garments among themselves in 19:23–24.

John 19:1–13 is something of a two-part chiasm, with verse 8 serving as a hinge between the two. This section can be depicted as follows:

19:1–8, 8–13, Behold the Man, Pilate Sought to Release

19:1, Then Pilate took
 19:2–3, King of the Jews
  19:4, Pilate: "I find no guilt in him"
   19:5a, Crown of thorns; purple robe
    19:5b, Behold the man
   19:6a, Crucify!
  19:6b, Pilate: "I find no guilt in him"
 19:7, Son of God
19:8–9, When Pilate heard and went in to the praetorium
 19:10, Pilate: "I have authority to release you"
  19:11, Jesus: "You would have no authority . . ."
 19:12, Pilate sought to release him
19:13, Pilate heard and went out to the judgment seat

The central statement of the first part at 19:5b, "Behold the man" (ESV), is strikingly similar to the central statements in the chiastic structure of John 19:23–30, "Behold, your son," and "Behold, your mother" (19:26–27 ESV).

19:23–30, Scripture Fulfilled, It Is Finished

19:23–24a, When they crucified Jesus, they took
 19:24b, That the Scripture might be fulfilled that says
  19:25–26a, His mother and the disciple whom he loved
   19:26b, Woman, behold your son

19:27a, Behold your mother
19:27b, He took her to his own home
19:28–29, That the Scripture might be accomplished, he says
19:30, When Jesus took the sour wine

The fact that Pilate finds no guilt in Jesus (19:4, 6b), and that Jesus refused to answer Pilate (19:9–10), means that what took place fulfilled Isaiah 53:7–9,

> He was oppressed, and he was afflicted,
> yet he opened not his mouth;
> like a lamb that is led to the slaughter,
> and like a sheep that before its shearers is silent,
> so he opened not his mouth.
> By oppression and judgment he was taken away; . . .
> although he had done no violence,
> and there was no deceit in his mouth. (ESV)

John does not explicitly call attention to these fulfillments, but he narrates the events in such a way that readers familiar with Isaiah 53 can hardly fail to see the connections. And these stand across from the way John calls attention to the fulfillment of Psalm 22:18 in John 19:24 and Psalm 69:21 in John 19:28. Isaiah seems to have referenced Psalms 22 and 69 in his fifty-third chapter,[2] so it seems fitting that John would place allusions to Isaiah 53 across from fulfillments of Psalms 22 and 69 in his chiastic structure, immediately framing his account of Jesus being crucified.

John presents Jesus as the suffering servant who fulfills the patterns David typified in Psalms 22 and 69, patterns Isaiah prophesied in Isaiah 53.

2. James M. Hamilton Jr., *Typology—Understanding the Bible's Promise-Shaped Patterns: How Old Testament Expectations Are Fulfilled in Christ* (Grand Rapids: Zondervan, 2022), 203–7.

19:14–22, Crucified

John's amazingly balanced statements can be seen in the summary of the chiastic structure of his crucifixion account, whose bare simplicity slows the reader down and imposes solemn reflection.

19:14–22, The Crucified King of the Jews

19:14, Pilate: "Behold your king"

 19:15, Shall I crucify your king?

  19:16, He handed him over to be crucified

   19:17, The Place of the Skull, Golgotha

  19:18, They crucified him

 19:19–20, Pilate's inscription: "king of the Jews"

19:21–22, Do not write "king of the Jews"

The central statement of this structure references the skull and the place name, Golgotha, in John 19:17. The name Golgotha appears to reference a Hebrew word for "head" or "skull," גֻּלְגֹּלֶת, referring to the crushing of the serpent's head first prophesied in Genesis 3:15 (though it should be observed that Gen. 3:15 has the synonymous term for "head," רֹאשׁ).

At the cross Christ cast out the ruler of this world (John 12:31), crushing the serpent's head by his death.

John 2–4 and 18–20

Both John 2–4 and John 18–20 have references to the season of Passover and key events that happen on the third day: Jesus cleansed the temple in Jerusalem (2:13–25) at the time of the Passover (2:13). John presents Jesus being crucified on "the day of Preparation for the Passover" (19:14, 31, 42). Jesus turned the water to wine (2:1–12) "on the third day" (2:1), and he healed the official's son (4:43–54) "after the two days" he had stayed with the Samaritans (4:43). John does not explicitly name "the first day of the week" (20:1) on which Jesus was raised "the third day," but it was just that.

John seems to have linked these two units of his Gospel (chaps. 2–4; 18–20) to each other by means of the references to the disciples not understanding the Scripture until the resurrection:

- "When therefore he was raised from the dead, his disciples remembered that he had said this, and they believed the Scripture and the word that Jesus had spoken" (2:22 ESV).
- "For as yet they did not understand the Scripture, that he must rise from the dead" (20:9 ESV).

The only other instance of a statement like this in John comes near the center of the Gospel, at 12:16, "His disciples did not understand these things at first, but when Jesus was glorified, then they remembered that these things had been written about him and had been done to him" (ESV). One of these statements comes in the second section of the Gospel, the next one comes in the middle, and the third comes in the second-to-last section.

Another fascinating point of contact between John 2–4 and John 18–20 comes in the first section of the first, the account of Jesus changing water to wine in 2:1–12, and in the last section of the second, when Jesus encounters Mary in the garden in 20:12–18. In each of these, Jesus responds to the female named Mary by addressing her as "Woman" and continuing with a question:

- "Woman, what does this have to do with me?" (2:4 ESV)
- "Woman, why are you weeping? Whom are you seeking?" (20:15 ESV)

Along with the other features discussed here (Passover, third day, understanding Scripture after the resurrection), these very similar exchanges were intended to associate these narratives. John wanted his audience to think of the narrative section that runs from Cana to Cana in John 2–4 when encountering the narrative section that runs from garden to garden in John 18:1–20:18.

We observed above the way the second question Jesus asked Mary, "Whom are you seeking?" (20:15 ESV), links up with Jesus asking the same question of Judas and his cohort in 18:4. Readers who reflect on the end of John in light of the beginning will likely also recall Jesus asking the disciples of the Baptist a similar question in 1:38, which the ESV renders, "Jesus turned and saw them following and said to them, 'What are you seeking?' And they said to him, 'Rabbi' (which means Teacher), 'where are you staying?'" This passage is remarkably similar to John 20:15–16, the relevant parts of which the ESV renders, "'Whom are you seeking?' . . . Jesus said to her, 'Mary.' She turned and said to him in Aramaic, 'Rabboni!' (which means Teacher)" (cf. 1:45; 4:27). This serves with other features of the end of John's Gospel to point back to its beginning, as will be discussed in the next chapter.

The most significant point of contact between John 2–4 and 18–20 is the way that in the first, speaking of the temple of his body (2:21) in John 2:19, "Jesus answered them, 'Destroy this temple, and in three days I will raise it up'" (ESV). Then in the second, those very things happen: The temple of Jesus' body is torn down when he is crucified in John 19:14–22, and he raises it up on the third day as narrated in John 20:1–18. As with the miracles John narrates in 2–4 (water to wine, raising of the official's son), the resurrection in 18–20 itself is not directly narrated (contrast the way Lazarus is described coming out of the tomb in 11:44). Jesus is buried at the end of John 19, and the tomb is empty at the beginning of John 20, with Peter and the other disciple finding the graveclothes in 20:6–7, Mary then encountering the risen Lord in 20:14.

The temple's significance and ministry have been fulfilled in the incarnation, crucifixion, and resurrection, and the empty tomb, like the Holy of Holies, can be entered because of what Christ has done (20:6, 8, 11–12). Even when Mary, no high priest on the Day of Atonement, looks into the tomb, the cherubim-style angels at the head and foot of where Jesus' body lay pose no threat to her. They only ask why she weeps (20:13). They know the night of weeping is over: The morn of rejoicing has come.

EXCURSUS: PROPOSED CHIASTIC STRUCTURES FOR JOHN 18:1–20:18

Chiastic structures for John 19:1–13, 14–22, and 23–30 appeared in the body of this chapter. Here are proposed structures for the other units of this section:

18:1–11, Jesus Arrested in a Garden

18:1, Having said these things, Jesus

  18:2–3, Judas and his cohort

    18:4, Whom do you seek?

      18:5, He says to them: I Am

      18:6, When he said to them: I Am

    18:7–9, Whom do you seek?

  18:10, Peter and his sword

18:11, Then Jesus said

18:12–28, Peter and the Other Disciple Follow Jesus

18:12–14, They led Jesus to Annas

  18:15–18, Simon Peter; you also are one of his disciples; I am not; standing and warming themselves

    18:19–21, High priest questioned; Jesus answered him . . . Why?

    18:22–24, Officer struck; Jesus answered him . . . Why?

  18:25–27, Simon Peter standing and warming himself; you also are one of his disciples; I am not

18:28, They led Jesus from Caiaphas

18:29–40, Pilate and the Innocent King of the Jews

18:29–31, Pilate and the Jews: What charge?

18:32, To fulfill the word that Jesus had spoken

18:33, Are you the king of the Jews?

18:34, Jesus answered . . .

18:35, Your people and the high priest handed you over

18:36, Jesus answered . . .

18:37a, So you are a king?

18:37b–38a, To bear witness to the truth

18:38b–40, Pilate and the Jews: No guilt in him

See within the chapter for 19:1–30.

19:31–42, No Broken Bones, Pierced, Scripture Fulfilled

19:31a, The day of Preparation, Sabbath . . . Sabbath

19:31b–33, The Jews asked Pilate to break legs

19:34, Pierced

19:35, True testimony

19:36, Scripture fulfilled

19:37, Pierced

19:38–40, Joseph asks Pilate for Jesus' body

19:42, Garden . . . garden, the day of Preparation

20:1–11, Peter and the Other Disciple Run to the Tomb

20:1, First day of the week, Mary comes to the tomb

20:2a, Mary runs to Simon Peter and the other disciple

20:2b, The Lord out of the tomb, and we do not know where

20:3–4, Peter and the other disciple, who came first to the tomb

20:5, He stooped to look but did not enter

20:6–7, Peter enters and sees graveclothes

20:8a, Then the other disciple entered

20:8b, The one who reached the tomb first

20:9, They did not know the Scripture that he must rise (cf. 2:22)

20:10, The disciples went again to them

20:11, Mary weeping at the tomb

20:11–18, Mary and Jesus in the Garden

20:11–12, Mary Magdalene weeping at tomb sees two angels

20:13, They have taken away my Lord

20:14, She turned and did not recognize Jesus

20:15a, Who are you seeking? (cf. 18:4; 1:38, 45; 4:27)

20:15b, She thought he was the gardener

20:16a, Jesus said to her, "Mary"

20:16b, She turned and recognized Jesus (Rabbi, cf. 1:38)

20:17, I ascend to my Father

20:18, Mary Magdalene angels (i.e., acts as a messenger) to the disciples

Questions for Reflection and Discussion

1. What conclusions can be drawn from the placement of the three places John notes that the disciples later remembered or understood what Jesus said or did (2:22; 12:16; 20:9)?
2. We have not thought deeply enough about the evil of our sin, and we have not yet realized the power of God's love

for sinners. From John 18:1–20:18, what stands out to you about the sinfulness of man and the love of God in Christ?

Suggested Reading

Bauckham, Richard. *The Theology of the Book of Revelation*. New Testament Theology. New York: Cambridge University Press, 1993.

Sailhamer, John. "The Messiah and the Hebrew Bible." *Journal of the Evangelical Theological Society* 44 (2001): 5–23.

Williams, Peter J. *Can We Trust the Gospels?* Wheaton: Crossway, 2018.

8

THE TEMPLE OF THE HOLY SPIRIT

Jesus Sends as He Was Sent in John 20:19–21:25

> The Word was alive even when his holy flesh was tasting death,
> so that when death was beaten and corruption trodden underfoot
> the power of the resurrection might come upon the whole human race.
>
> —Cyril of Alexandria, *On the Unity of Christ*[1]

The end of John's Gospel recalls its beginning, lands its story arc, and anticipates the way the disciples will continue the ministry of Jesus. The one on whom the Spirit came down to remain at the beginning (1:29–34) imparts the same Spirit to his disciples at the end (20:22–23).

1. Cyril of Alexandria, *On the Unity of Christ*, trans. John Anthony McGuckin (Crestwood, NY: St. Vladimir's Seminary Press, 1995), 115.

Consider too the corresponding elements of the final section of John's Gospel: The witness-bearing Spirit at the beginning of this unit (20:22) is the same Spirit Jesus said would lead his disciples into all truth (16:13), and at unit's end the witness-bearing disciple asserts the truthfulness of his testimony (21:24).

In second and second-to-last positions the resurrected Lord convinces doubting Thomas by the proofs of his hands and side (20:24–29), and that same resurrected Lord restores Peter to ministry (21:15–23). These corresponding units show the convincing and restoring power of the risen Christ.

At the center of this unit stand two statements that point to the way the followers of Jesus will seek to bring others to Jesus (cf. 17:20). First, John asserts in 20:30–31 that he writes so that his audience will believe and thereby have life. Second, the miraculous catch of fish in John 21:1–14 functions like other miracles in John to point beyond itself to what it signifies, which is that now the followers of Jesus are to be fishers of men.

The chiastic structure of this final section of John's Gospel, which corresponds to the Gospel's first chapter, can be depicted as follows:

20:19–23, As the Father sent me
    20:24–29, Thomas believes
        20:30–31, John writes for his audience to believe
        21:1–14, Going fishing
    21:15–23, Peter restored; feed my sheep
21:24–25, True testimony and unlimited books

In this discussion we will begin at the center of this chiastic structure and work out to its edges.

20:30–31 and 21:1–14, Evangelistic Purpose and a Fishing Trip

As we have seen throughout this project, John took great care in the writing of his Gospel, in whole and in part, planning, structuring, and intentionally arranging to maximize his communicative force. As he comes to this his concluding section, he centers his purpose statement and an illustration of the same, placing John 20:30–31 and 21:1–14 in the central position of the final chiastic structure of his chiastic book.

In John 20:30–31 John says two things: first, that Jesus did many other signs, which his disciples witnessed, and second, that he, John, wrote these so that his audience might believe that Jesus is the Messiah, the Son of God, and that believing they might have life in his name. Hereby John indicates that in his Gospel he seeks to go as he has been sent (cf. 20:21), to serve as he has been served (13:14–16), to love as he has been loved (15:12). He seeks to bear the fruit for which Jesus chose and appointed his disciples (15:16). Jesus prayed for those who would believe through the word of his disciples (17:20), and in his Gospel John proclaims a word written that others might believe.

As we turn to the catch of fish in John 21:1–14, a review of the chiastic structure of the passage will remind readers of its content:

21:1–14, The Fishing Trip

21:1, Jesus manifested himself to the disciples

  21:2, Disciples named (cf. 1:35–42)

    21:3, Simon Peter and disciples embark to the boat, catch nothing

      21:4, The disciples did not know that "it was Jesus"

        21:5, Jesus asks if they have food; "They answered no" (cf. 1:21)

          21:6a, Jesus tells them to throw the net

        21:6b, They throw and cannot drag the net for all the fish

      21:7–8, Disciples recognize that "it is the Lord"

21:9–11, Simon Peter and disciples disembark to the land, bring catch

21:12–13, Jesus summons disciples (cf. 1:19)

21:14, Jesus manifested himself to the disciples

Matthew 4 indicates that right after calling Peter and Andrew and telling them he would make them fishers of men (Matt. 4:18–20), Jesus called the sons of Zebedee (4:21–22). Luke 5 similarly relates that after a great catch of fish, Simon "and all who were with him were astonished, . . . and so also were James and John, sons of Zebedee, who were partners with Simon. And Jesus said to Simon, 'Do not be afraid; from now on you will be catching men'" (5:9–10 ESV). These texts reflect the influence of Jeremiah 16, where having prophesied the exile in 16:1–13, Jeremiah points to the new exodus in 16:14–15. Through Jeremiah the Lord then declares how he will bring back the scattered people in 16:16, "Behold, I am sending for many fishers, declares the Lord, and they shall catch them" (ESV). The words of Jesus making his disciples "fishers of men" in Matthew 4 and Luke 5, then, point to the fulfillment of Jeremiah 16:16.

I would suggest that similar things are at work in John 21:1–14, and that the miraculous catch of fish here functions the same way other miracles in John have. Jesus turned water into wine in John 2:1–12, and that best wine pointed forward to the new covenant but was not, literally speaking, the covenant itself. Jesus healed the official's son in John 4:43–54, and then he healed the man at the Pool of Bethesda in 5:1–18, topping those with the resurrection of Lazarus from the dead in 11:1–44. The healings pointed to deliverance from the effects of sin through the restoration of resurrection, and the raising of Lazarus from the dead did the same, but neither the healings nor the raising of Lazarus were, literally speaking, the realization of the defeat of death anticipated at Christ's return (cf. 5:21, 28–29). Jesus fed the five thousand in John 6, but as he indicates in 6:27, the food he gave the people was not "the food that endures to eternal life" (ESV). The point in all these instances, and it can also be said of the giving of sight to the man born blind in John 9, is that what Jesus does points beyond itself to the hoped-for fulfillment. The wine from the water signifies a new covenant, the healings and the raising of Lazarus point to the resurrection, and the provision of food points to the bread of life, "he who comes down from heaven and gives life to the world" (6:33 ESV).

Read in the context of the other signs in John's Gospel, then, I would suggest that the great catch of fish functions the same way the others do, and the exact number of fish, 153 (21:11), functions like the detail of there being "five thousand in number" (6:10) with "twelve baskets" of leftovers (6:13). Just as the feeding pointed beyond itself to what Christ would provide in himself, so the catch points beyond itself to the way the disciples would succeed as fishers of men. The opportunity to proclaim the kingdom to the Samaritans is spoken of with similar imagery though from a different sphere. In John 4 as the Samaritans make their way to Jesus, he speaks of fields white for harvest, of sowing and reaping, and of entering into the labor of others (4:35–38). The great catch of fish in John 21 signifies that the disciples will go on to be the fishers of men Jesus says they will be in other Gospels, just as the book of Acts narrates.

There are also a number of statements in John 21:1–14 that recall the way the disciples first came to Jesus back in John 1:35–51.

- The Baptist came that Jesus might be "revealed to Israel" in 1:31 (cf. also 2:11), and Jesus "revealed himself again to the disciples" in 21:1 (cf. 21:14; 20:19–23 and 24–29).
- The Baptist was there with "two of his disciples" in 1:35, and the exact same phrase (ἐκ τῶν μαθητῶν αὐτοῦ δύο) appears in John 21:2. These are the only two instances of the phrase in John's Gospel.

- Simon Peter and Nathanael are named in 1:35–51 and in 21:2, and in both John 1 and 21 there is a smaller group of disciples, five are enumerated in John 1, seven in John 21.
- The question and the phrase, "They answered him, 'No'" in 21:5 is worded very similarly to the exchange between the priests and Levites and the Baptist in 1:21, "And he answered, 'No.'"
- John relates in 21:12, "None of the disciples dared ask him, 'Who are you?'" And the "who are you" question is worded exactly as it was when posed to the Baptist in 1:19.
- With these other reminiscences of John 1, the "It is the Lord!" in 21:7 recalls the "We have found the Messiah" sentiments at 1:41 and 1:45.

These callbacks to John 1 indicate that just as the disciples were speaking of Jesus and bringing others to him at the beginning of John's Gospel, the allusions to the beginning and the catch of fish at the end indicate they will continue as ambassadors for Christ beyond the pages of John's narrative (cf. 2 Cor. 5:20).

20:24–29 and 21:15–23, Convincing and Restoring Power

The point of contact between John 20:24–29 and 21:15–23 seems to be the power of the risen Christ to inspire belief and restore the fallen. In 20:24–29 Thomas, who had not yet seen the risen Lord, communicates his profound skepticism about the resurrection, which Jesus overcomes by appearing to the disciples and directly addressing the concerns Thomas articulated. In 21:15–23, the Peter who denied Jesus three times is given three opportunities to affirm his love for Jesus, and then Jesus tells him that he, Peter, will be faithful until death.

A presentation of the chiastic structure of John 20:24–29 will afford a quick review of the passage:

20:24–29, Thomas Believes

20:24, Thomas was not there

20:25a, We have seen the Lord

20:25b, Unless I see his hands and touch his side

20:26, Eight days later: Peace be with you (cf. 20:19 and 21)

20:27, See my hands and touch my side

20:28, My Lord and my God!

20:29, Have you believed because you have seen me? (cf. 1:50)

This episode makes a number of important points. First, we see that the disciples did not believe in the resurrection simply because they were uncritical thinkers who would gullibly believe any claim made. Rather, Thomas is clearly evaluating the claims made by his friends and requiring evidence that will satisfy the demands of credulity. He wants physical proof that Jesus has been bodily raised in history. At a specific point in time, eight days later (20:26), Jesus comes and speaks the words he had spoken in his previous resurrection appearance (20:19, 21).

In this resurrection appearance Jesus appears in ways both natural and supernatural, human and divine. In verse 26, though the doors are locked, he is able to enter the room. Then in verse 27, though he was not present to hear what Thomas said in verse 25, he knows and addresses those statements in exacting detail. These features of the account point to the divine, supernatural, resurrected glory of the Lord Jesus. On the other hand, he also remains human. He will eat breakfast with the disciples in 21:12–15, he now stands among them in 20:26, and his human body bears the marks of having been crucified in 20:27.

All this convinces Thomas, who hails Jesus as Lord and God, in response to which Jesus says words in 20:29 that recall 1:50.

- "Jesus answered him, 'Because I said to you, "I saw you under the fig tree," do you believe? You will see greater things than these'" (1:50 ESV).
- "Jesus said to him, 'Have you believed because you have seen me? Blessed are those who have not seen and yet have believed'" (20:29 ESV).

The statement in John 20, at almost the very end of the Gospel, clearly evokes 1:50, near its beginning, and in both cases Jesus responds to faith with a question, then points to more in the future. In the case of John 1:50, he tells Nathanael that he will see greater things, likely alluding to the things John goes on to narrate in his Gospel. In the case of 20:29, those who have not seen and yet believed are those who will hear of Jesus from Thomas and the other disciples.

John presents his Gospel such that Jesus speaks with certainty about those who will be convinced by the proofs given to Thomas that Jesus was bodily raised from the dead. Jesus was raised, and he has the power to convince those skeptical of that fact.

As we turn to Jesus charging Peter to feed his sheep, here again a presentation of the chiastic structure of the passage will allow for a quick summary of its contents:

21:15–23, Peter Restored

21:15, Simon, do you love me more than these? Feed my lambs

  21:16, A second time: Tend my sheep

    21:17, A third time: Feed my sheep

      21:18, Where you do not want to go

        21:19, Signifying by what kind of death Peter would glorify God: Follow me

      21:20, Peter turned and saw the disciple Jesus loved

21:21, What about this man?
21:22, If it is my will that he remain: Follow me
21:23, If it is my will that he remain

The glorious uniqueness of the Bible's good news is on display in this narrative. Peter had committed himself to Jesus, proclaimed his faith that Jesus was the expected Messiah, and promised even to die for Jesus. And then he failed. Non-Christian approaches to life would be honor bound to regard Peter as a disappointment. He would not be trusted. There would be no forgiveness for him. He had proven himself unreliable.

In the remarkable account that closes John's Gospel, I would propose that verse 19, where John explains that Jesus has spoken of the martyr's death by which Peter will glorify God, stands central. This means that the faithless one not only will be given another opportunity to show himself faithful but that because of the power of the word of Jesus and the Spirit he gives, the one who showed himself faithless will *be* faithful unto death. Here is hope for all who have failed, redemption for all who have been enslaved by their sin (cf. 8:34). And though it is not explicitly articulated in the words of the passage, Jesus has clearly forgiven Peter.

Peter is not defined by his failure. Whereas Judas is everywhere in the Gospel identified as the one who betrayed Jesus, Peter is not identified as the one who denied him but as "Simon, son of John" (21:15). In the opening and closing verses of this unit, Jesus makes enigmatic statements as he defines Peter's identity. In the first, Jesus calls Peter by name and asks him if he loves him (Jesus) "more than these" (21:15). The enigmatic part has to do with the referent of the demonstrative pronoun "these." Is Jesus asking Peter if he loves him more than the fish that have just been taken (21:11), signifying his work as a fisherman? Is Jesus asking Peter if he thinks his love for Jesus is stronger than that of the others present, who were named in 21:2? Or is Jesus asking Peter if Peter loves Jesus more than he loves those other people? In view of Peter's denials, the second option seems to me the least likely, but whatever the case, the key thing is this: Jesus is affording to Peter the opportunity to be defined as someone who loves Jesus.

Peter's family of origin is affirmed (son of John), his love for Jesus is affirmed (Do you love me?), and his service for Jesus is affirmed (Feed my lambs). Peter will not be defined by his failure but by his identity as a son of John who loves Jesus and shepherds the people of Jesus. And this will culminate in his self-sacrificial Christlike death to glorify God (21:19).

In the closing words of this unit Peter has asked about the beloved disciple, and the words Jesus has spoken about *his will* for that man are reaffirmed. These words challenge Peter to be a man who accepts the will of Jesus.

The intervening verses build out these big ideas. In John 21:16–17, Jesus asks Peter twice more if he loves him, twice more charging him with pastoral responsibility, thus matching Peter's three denials with three affirmations of love and three commands to shepherd. John 21:18 then outlines the way that Peter will be cruciform and Christlike in his death, 21:19 making that plain by authorial explanation and a final call from Jesus to Peter: "Follow me." From that centerpoint the challenge to embrace Christ's will for him personally develops as Peter sees the beloved disciple, asks about him, and hears the Lord's response in John 21:20–22.

The power of the resurrected Christ enables him to overcome the doubts of skeptics like Thomas and redefine the identity of failures like Peter.

20:19–23 and 21:24–25, Spirit-Led, True Testimony

We come to the first and last units of the final section of John's Gospel, which seem to enact John 15:26–27. In John 20:19–23, the risen Christ imparts the Spirit to his disciples, setting in motion the realization of what he described in John 15:26, "But when the Helper comes, whom I will send to you from the Father, the Spirit of truth, who proceeds from the Father, he will bear witness about me" (ESV). Then in John 21:24–25, John asserts the truth of his witness-bearing testimony, proving out the words Jesus spoke in John 15:27, "And you also will bear witness, because you have been with me from the beginning" (ESV).

The chiastic structure of John 20:19–23 can be depicted as follows:

20:19–23, As the Father Sent Me

20:19a, First day of the week

  20:19b, Peace be with you

    20:20, He showed them his hands and side

  20:21, Peace be with you; as the Father sent me I send you

20:22–23, Receive the Holy Spirit

Starting at the center of this unit and moving outward through its concentric statements will bring out the import of what John portrays here.

Jesus has been raised from the dead. The one who is the Word, God and with God in the beginning (1:1), whom the Father consecrated and sent into the world (10:36), the Word who became flesh (1:14), the God-man Jesus (10:30), who was crucified, dead, and buried (19:18, 33, 42), that man stands raised from the dead before his disciples, showing them his pierced hands and side (20:20a). In perhaps the greatest understatement in the entirety of the Bible, John comments, "Then the disciples were glad when they saw the Lord" (20:20b ESV). They had recognized him as the Messiah. They saw him raise Lazarus from the dead. Then he was crucified. How to describe their hopes at that point? A smoking ruin. Dust and ashes. Sackcloth. Cratered expectation. But then though the doors were locked (20:19a), he entered, spoke peace (20:19b), and proved his identity by showing them his hands and side (20:20a). Then the understatement: They saw him and were glad. Indeed.

Precisely because it really was him ("his hands and his side"), because of what his death and resurrection accomplished, he can speak the words that frame verse 20, "Peace be with you" (ESV), in 20:19b and 20:21a. Because the disciples have been reconciled to God through the death and resurrection of Jesus, they have peace with God (cf. Rom. 5:1). Because of that, Jesus can send the disciples as the Father sent him (John 20:21b).

For Jesus to send the disciples as the Father sent him, the disciples must have the Holy Spirit, just as Jesus had the Holy Spirit (1:29–34). We will revisit this topic in chapter 10 below, but here we observe the progression: The Father gave the Spirit to Jesus. Jesus fulfilled his earthly mission. Jesus then gave the Spirit to his disciples, who have a mission to undertake.

Jesus came as the fulfillment of the temple (see discussions of John 1 and 2–4 above). As such, he was the place where God was present and where sin was dealt with. Now that he has fulfilled the sacrificial system of the temple by his death and resurrection, he can impart the Spirit to the disciples and make them a temple where no sacrifices for sin need to be offered. The disciples of Jesus become the place where God is present by means of the Spirit, and where sin is dealt with because they communicate the message that forgiveness is available. Forgiveness is only possible for those who are in Christ. Only the disciples of Jesus are authorized by Jesus to continue the ministry of Jesus. Thus the words of Jesus to them: "If you forgive the sins of any, they are forgiven them; if you withhold forgiveness from any, it is withheld" (20:23 ESV).

Because he accomplished the work the Father gave him to do in his life and on the cross (17:4; 19:30), Jesus can speak peace to his disciples (20:19b, 21a), impart the Spirit to them (16:7; 20:22), and authorize them to forgive and retain sin (20:23). As the Father sent him, he sends them.

The Spirit came down on Jesus to remain upon him at the beginning of John's Gospel (1:29–34), and he imparts the Spirit to his disciples at its end (20:22). Jesus asked Nathanael if he believed because of what he said to him at the beginning (1:50), and he made a similar statement to Thomas at the end (20:29). The disciples of the Baptist were with him by the Jordan River when they recognized Jesus at the beginning (1:19–37), and the disciples of Jesus recognize him by the Sea of Tiberias at the end (21:1–14). Jesus calls Peter "Simon, son of John" at beginning and end (1:42; 21:15).

In addition to these correspondences between the beginning and end of John's Gospel, there are important ways in which the final two verses of John's Gospel, 21:24–25, correspond to John 1:1–18. Here again a summary of the chiastic shape of John's closing comments allows us to review their contents:

21:24–25, John's True Testimony

21:24a, This is the disciple who bears witness concerning these things

  21:24b, And who has written these things

    21:24c, And we know that his witness is true

    21:25a, And there are many other things that Jesus did

  21:25b, Which if they were written one by one

21:25c, I suppose not even the world itself would encompass the books that would be written

The testimony of John the Baptist is strategically interposed in the chiastic structure of John 1:1–18 at 1:6–8 and 1:15. John the Baptist's testimony at the beginning is matched by John son of Zebedee's testimony at the end, as he asserts in 21:24, "This is the disciple who is bearing witness about these things, and who has written these things, and we know that his testimony is true" (ESV). The Baptist "came as a witness, to bear witness about the light, that all might believe through him" (1:7 ESV), and the evangelist wrote "so that you may believe that Jesus is the Christ" (20:31), bearing true witness to the truth (21:24).

The Gospel opened with the affirmation of the word as God (1:1–2), through whom all was made: "All things were made through him, and without him was not any thing made that was made" (1:3 ESV). This is required for John 21:25 to be true: "Now there are also many other things that Jesus did. Were every one of them to be written, I suppose that the world itself could not contain the books that would be written" (ESV).

Is it the case that the world could not contain the books detailing the deeds of a merely human life? Does John 21:25 not require unlimited, infinited accomplishments?

John closes his Gospel in 21:25 with words that point back to its opening, where he spoke of the Word that was God and was with God in the beginning, through whom all was made, in whom was life, life that was light that darkness cannot overcome (1:1–4), the only begotten God, in the bosom of the Father, making him known in the fullness of grace and truth that fulfills the law of Moses (1:14–18). Of this one alone can it be said that the world could not contain the books detailing all he has ever done (21:25).

Conclusion

John intended chapters 5–11 to stand across from chapters 12–17, and chapters 2–4 to stand across from 18:1–20:18. Similarly, it seems that John wrote 20:19–21:25 to stand across from 1:1–51, and the following proposed chiastic structure brings out the points of contact between the opening and closing units of John's Gospel:

1:1–51 and 20:19–21:25

1:1–18, The only begotten Word made flesh

  1:6–8, 15, The Baptist's testimony

    1:1–51, The fulfillment of the temple filled with the Spirit

20:19–21:25, The new temple filled with the Spirit
21:24, The evangelist's testimony
21:25, The world could not contain the books

Questions for Reflection and Discussion

1. What do you think of the suggestion that the catch of 153 fish should be read like the other "signs" in John's Gospel? Have you heard other explanations of the exact number?
2. People sometimes suggest that if the disciples are baptized in the Holy Spirit on the day of Pentecost (Acts 2), the giving of the Spirit in John 20:22 can only be "parabolic." But are these accounts describing the same thing? How are they similar, and how do they differ?
3. Thomas employs his critical thinking skills when he demands evidence that Jesus has indeed been raised from the dead. What stands out to you about how Jesus responds to the skepticism of Thomas and about the way Thomas responds when he sees the risen Christ?

Suggested Reading

Augustine. *The Trinity*. In *The Works of Saint Augustine: A Translation for the 21st Century*, translated by Edmund Hill. Brooklyn, NY: New City, 1991.

Irenaeus. *On the Apostolic Preaching*. Translated by John Behr. Popular Patristics Series. Crestwood, NY: St. Vladimir's Seminary Press, 1997.

Hamilton, James M., Jr. "Were Old Covenant Believers Indwelt by the Holy Spirit?" *Themelios* 30 (2004): 12–22.

9

THE WORD BECAME FLESH

The Incarnation in the Gospel of John

> For the whole Christ assumed the whole me
> that he might grant salvation to the whole me,
> for what is unassumable is incurable.
>
> —John of Damascus, *The Orthodox Faith* 3.6[1]

To this point in this book we have considered John's own structuring of his material to arrive at the message and theology of the Gospel bearing his name. The literary structure of John's Gospel has determined the shape and content of this book. As we turn to consider the incarnation in this chapter and the Trinity in the next, I am going to take guidance from Fred Sanders, who gives this advice for ordering discussions such as these: "Follow the leading ideas of the ecumenical councils of the

1. Quoted in Herman Bavinck, *Reformed Dogmatics*, ed. John Bolt, trans. John Vriend, vol. 3, *Sin and Salvation in Christ* (Grand Rapids: Baker Academic, 2006), 297.

early church and then support them with biblical argumentation."[2] This discussion will slot the Athanasian Creed in where Sanders has "the ecumenical councils." The creed, which is referred to as Athanasian not because Athanasius composed it but because it represents his theology,[3] has two recognizable parts, the first on the Trinity, the second on the incarnation, making it suitable for the limited scope of this project. When recently giving close attention to the Athanasian Creed, I became convinced that its two parts are each chiastically structured, which adds to its fitness for consideration here.[4]

When considered by biblical scholars, topics like the incarnation and the Trinity are usually discussed as though the authors of the New Testament did not yet have the doctrines fully crystalized in their thinking. Discussing Hebrews, R. B. Jamieson has noted, "Much study of the New Testament's Christology posits a basically evolutionary scheme of development. On this account, the earliest Christians did not believe that Jesus was divine; that gap was crossed later, perhaps much later."[5] This evolutionary scheme would fit with the notion that in the New Testament we have but the building blocks of the doctrines of the incarnation and the Trinity, not the finished edifices. On the basis of his argument

2. Fred Sanders, "Biblical Grounding for the Christology of the Councils," *Criswell Theological Review* 13 (2015): 93.

3. It seems to have been composed in Latin, and Athanasius wrote in Greek. See further J. N. D. Kelly, *The Athanasian Creed—Quicunque Vult: The Paddock Lectures for 1962–3* (Edinburgh: Adam & Charles Black, 1964).

4. See James M. Hamilton Jr., "The Chiastic Structure of the Athanasian Creed," *Journal of the Evangelical Theological Society* 66 (2023): 279–300. It has been suggested that the creed was heavily influenced by, and perhaps even quotes, Augustine, whose work *On the Trinity* is also chiastically structured. See Edmund Hill's explanation of the chiastic structure of Augustine's work in his introduction to *The Trinity* in *The Works of Saint Augustine: A Translation for the 21st Century*, trans. Edmund Hill (Brooklyn, NY: New City, 1991), 26–27. Hill observes of the Athanasian Creed, "It could much more justly be called the Augustinian Creed" (*The Trinity*, 47).

5. R. B. Jamieson, *The Paradox of Sonship: Christology in the Epistle to the Hebrews*, Studies in Christian Doctrine and Scripture (Downers Grove, IL: InterVarsity), 143–44.

from Hebrews, however, Jamieson contends that what that author writes "suggests not the rough edges of a new breakthrough but the orderly exposition of an achieved synthesis."[6] Jamieson further contends that "the critical construct of development from lower to higher is a singularly inapt, even distorting, lens through which to read Hebrews."[7] As I have tested Jamieson's hypothesis against John's Gospel, my conclusion is that John too writes from "an achieved synthesis."

The claim here is not that in his Gospel John uses the terminology that we find in the later creeds. As Fred Sanders observes, "The church has always known that the doctrine of the Trinity is profoundly biblical and yet not straightforwardly taught in the Bible."[8] And yet Sanders can also affirm, "Trinitarianism is a gift of revelation before it is an achievement of the church."[9] To paraphrase David Yeago, though John and the creeds do not use the same language, they nevertheless say the same thing. Yeago's helpful explanation of the distinction between judgments and concepts is worth quoting at length:

> It is essential, in this context, to distinguish between *judgment* and the *conceptual terms* in which those judgment [*sic*] are rendered. We cannot concretely perform an act of judgment without employing some particular, contingent verbal and conceptual resources; judgment-making is an operation performed with words and concepts. At the same time, however, the same judgment can be rendered in a variety of conceptual terms, all of which may be informative about a particular judgment's force and implications. . . . This point is especially important when we ask about the relationship between the New Testament and later church teaching. Unity in teaching must be sought at the level of judgment and

6. Jamieson, *Paradox of Sonship*, 145.

7. Jamieson, *Paradox of Sonship*, 145.

8. Fred Sanders, *The Triune God*, New Studies in Dogmatics (Grand Rapids: Zondervan, 2016), 22.

9. Sanders, *Triune God*, 23.

> not at the level of concepts because discourse only *teaches*, makes claims that can be accepted or rejected, insofar as it passes and urges judgment. An inquiry that remains at the level of concepts . . . will never succeed in properly *raising the question* of the relation between New Testament and later church teaching.[10]

The claim of this chapter and the next is that though the Gospel according to John and the Athanasian Creed use different *conceptual resources*, they render the same *judgment* about the incarnation and the Trinity. As Bavinck puts it, "While Scripture does not speak the language of the later theology, materially it contains what the Christian church confesses in its doctrine of the two natures."[11] That is to say, the Athanasian Creed provides a faithful exposition of John's theology.

In what follows I will first present the second part of the Athanasian Creed on the incarnation in its chiastic shape, prefaced and followed by brief explanatory comments. From there the leading ideas of the creed will be considered in relationship to what John shows and tells in his Gospel.

Part 2 of the Athanasian Creed: The Incarnation

The whole of the Athanasian Creed is bracketed by statements of necessary belief. The creed begins and ends with claims that the things it asserts must be believed for salvation, and then its two major sections have necessary belief *inclusios* that frame their distinctive concerns. Note the statements in bold font about believing rightly and faithfully in the A and A′ lines in the text of the creed below. The right faith is confessed in the B line and rewarded in the B′. The third section, C, deals with the Son's having been begotten of the Father in eternity past and begotten

10. David S. Yeago, "The New Testament and the Nicene Dogma: A Contribution to the Recovery of Theological Exegesis," *Sewanee Theological Review* 45 (2002): 378–79 (italics in original).

11. Bavinck, *Reformed Dogmatics*, 3:298.

of his mother in the last days, and then the third-to-last section, C′, narrates his past and future comings. The D and D′ sections both treat Christ as God and man of a reasonable soul and human flesh (underlined statements are parallel), the latter reversing the order of the former. Framing the central affirmation of unity, the E and E′ lines both speak to the Godhead and the manhood (key terms in small caps) of Christ. The central statement of the creed is marked by the letter *F*, affirming that Christ has two natures but is one person.

Part 2 of the Athanasian Creed, indented to reflect its chiastic structure, reads as follows:[12]

A Furthermore it is necessary to everlasting salvation that one also **believe rightly** the Incarnation of our Lord Jesus Christ.

B For the right faith is that we believe and confess that our Lord Jesus Christ, the Son of God, is God and Man;

C God, of the substance of the Father, begotten before the worlds: born in the world;

D perfect <u>God</u>, and perfect <u>man</u>: of a <u>reasonable soul and human flesh</u> subsisting;

E equal to the Father, as touching his GODHEAD: and inferior to the Father, as touching his MANHOOD.

F Who although he be God and man, yet he is not two, but one Christ;

12. The translation of the Athanasian Creed that follows was developed for recitation in worship at Kenwood Baptist Church at Victory Memorial in Louisville, KY, in 2022. Matt Damico and I worked together, aiming at an NKJV-style update of the text of the creed from the 1662 *Book of Common Prayer*. For the creed in Latin, see Michael Martin, "Quicumque: Athanasian Creed," Thesaurus Precum Latinarum, April 1998, https://www.preces-latinae.org/thesaurus/Symbola/Quicumque.html.

E′ one, not by conversion of the GODHEAD into flesh, but by taking of the MANHOOD into God; one altogether, not by confusion of substance but by unity of person.

D′ For as the reasonable soul and flesh is one man, so God and man is one Christ.

C′ Who suffered for our salvation, descended to the dead, rose again on the third day from the dead. He ascended into heaven: he sits on the right hand of the Father, God Almighty, from whence he shall come to judge the quick and the dead. At whose coming all men shall rise again with their bodies and shall give account for their own works.

B′ And they that have done good shall go into life everlasting, and they that have done evil into everlasting fire.

A′ This is the true Christian faith. Anyone who does not **believe faithfully** cannot be saved.

The following attempts to summarize the big ideas of part 2 of the creed:

Necessary belief

Right faith confessed

Two natures (substances): God and man, eternally begotten of the Father, born in the world of his mother

Reasonable soul and human flesh

Godhead and manhood (equal and inferior)

Two natures one person

Godhead and manhood (not converted but added, distinct in nature, unified in person)

Reasonable soul and human flesh

Missions past and future: suffered, buried, rose, ascended, enthroned, returning to judge

Right life rewarded

Necessary belief

We will group the corresponding affirmations in the creed's chiastic structure (joining the first and last statements, second and second to last, and so on) to compare its teaching with John's, treating the following topics:

- Necessary belief
- Confession and rewards
- Begotten of the Father and born in the world
- Reasonable soul and human flesh
- Equal according to Godhead, inferior according to manhood
- One Christ

These bullet points constitute the subheads in the following discussion, and they are derived from the corresponding units of the summary of the chiasm above, starting at the outer edges (necessary belief) and working down (through right faith confessed and rewarded, etc.) to the center (two natures one person).

Necessary Belief

To feel the force of the words John presents Jesus saying, we must put them in the context of the Old Testament's absolute monotheism and Yahweh's jealous guarding of his own name. The declaration of Israel's faith in Deuteronomy 6:4 makes the first point: "Hear O Israel, Yahweh our God, Yahweh is one." Yahweh's own assertions in Isaiah 42:8 make the second: "I am Yahweh. That is my name. My glory to another I will not give." These claims stand in stark relief against the words of Jesus to the effect that he shared in his Father's glory before the world was made: "And now, glorify me, Father, with yourself with the glory that I had with you before the world was" (John 17:5). This is not the only time that John presents Jesus speaking of the Father sharing his glory with him (see esp. 13:32 and 17:1). In light of Yahweh saying in Isaiah 42:8 that he will not give his glory to another, it is especially striking that in John 17:22 Jesus speaks of "the glory which you gave to me." To paraphrase a question elsewhere in the Gospels: Who then is this, to whom Yahweh gives his own exclusive glory?[13]

It is important to stress that such questions are not imposed on the text from a foreign worldview being somehow layered onto the biblical material. Rather, the Old Testament itself makes exclusive statements that cannot be abandoned when we read other statements made in the New Testament. In addition to presenting Jesus claiming to share in Yahweh's exclusive glory that he gives to no other, John presents Jesus repeatedly asserting himself *as Yahweh*, declaring of himself (as Yahweh did in Exod. 3:14), "I Am." One of these, John 8:24, poignantly communicates the point under discussion here, which is that believing rightly and faithfully in the incarnation of the Lord Jesus Christ "is necessary to everlasting salvation." John presents Jesus saying in John 8:24, "Unless you believe that I Am, you will die in your sins" (for other "I Am" statements in John, see 4:26; 8:28; 13:19; 18:5, 6, 8).

In John's Gospel, Jesus asserts in John 8:24 that only those who believe that he himself is Yahweh will be saved from dying in their sins (cf. also 1:10–13; 3:36; 14:6).

Confession and Rewards

We saw in our discussion of John 5:19–30 that there is an intrinsic connection between *believing* what John presents about Jesus and the Father and *doing good*. From the literary structure

13. See the next chapter on the Trinity for the Spirit's involvement in giving glory to Christ in John 16:14.

of that passage, it is clear that "those who have done good" (ESV) in 5:29 are those who hear the words of Jesus and believe the one who sent him in 5:24. This complex of ideas entails believing that Jesus was sent from the Father, which entails him having been with the Father before being sent (cf. 10:36). It also requires acceptance of what Jesus says in the immediate context, where he asserts that his Father is working (on the Sabbath) and he is doing likewise (5:17), which John then makes plain was understood by his opponents as "calling God his own Father, making himself equal with God" (5:18 ESV).

We discussed above the way that Jesus claims in this passage to act in accordance with what the Father does because of his unique perception of the Father: He saw and heard the Father, and the Father granted him life in himself, resulting in power to raise the dead, along with authority to execute judgment (see chap. 5 above on 5:19–30). Jesus says that those who believe all this about his relationship with the Father—all that the Father gave to him, and thus how he is equal with the Father—those who believe these things "believe the one who sent" him and are not judged but have everlasting life (5:24). These same people are "the ones who have done good" and rise to life rather than judgment (5:29).

John's Gospel teaches that believing rightly leads to acting rightly (5:24, 29): To know the truth is to be set free from slavery to sin (8:34–36), and to love Jesus is to obey his commands (14:15, 21, 23–24). The revelation of God in Christ that comes about as Jesus speaks words of Spirit and life (6:63) transforms people in the same way that God's word of creation calls into being what did not exist before he spoke (5:25, 38; 6:68; 8:31; 15:3, 7; cf. Gen. 1:3; Rom. 4:17).

John presents Peter confessing that Jesus is the one who has the words of eternal life (John 6:68), and he notes when others refuse to confess him even though they apprehend the truth of what he says (9:22; 12:42–43). From the narrative, it is clear that John regards a refusal to confess Jesus as a refusal to speak what is true, a cowardly concession to the ruler of this world (12:31) and those pursuing his agenda (8:44). Those who believe will do good and identify with Jesus, even risking public exposure that could lead to the Jews and Romans treating them just as they did Jesus (see Joseph and Nicodemus burying Jesus in 19:38–42).

All this is concisely summarized by the second and second-to-last statements in the incarnation section of the Athanasian Creed (the B and B′ lines above). The first speaks of believing and confessing that Jesus is God and man, and the second speaks of doing good and entering everlasting life rather than everlasting fire. Those with ears to hear recognize a beautiful consonance between those two statements and John 5:24 and 5:29.

Begotten of the Father and Born in the World

As we take up consideration of Christ as begotten of both God his Father and Mary his mother, we must bear in mind a point well put by R. B. Jamieson: "The creeds do not solve riddles; they preserve mysteries."[14] That is to say, what the Athanasian Creed says about Jesus (in the C and C′ lines) being of the substance of his divine Father and his human mother, begotten of the former before the worlds and of the latter in the world, merely affirms what John says.

On the one hand, the Word was God and was with God in the beginning, and all things were made through him (1:1–3). That he is of the same substance as God is stated in the phrase "the Word was God" (1:1), implications of which are revealed in the affirmation "in him was life" (1:4). As to how all this came about, John describes Jesus as the "only begotten" of God the Father (1:14, 18; 3:16, 18), and he presents Jesus speaking of the Father "granting" the Son to have life in himself (5:26), of himself living "because of the Father" (6:57), and of speaking truth that he "heard from God" (8:40). All this sheds light on the eternal relations of origin

14. Jamieson, *Paradox of Sonship*, 152.

between the Father and the Son, and it all arises from what John and the other New Testament authors manifestly believe: first, that there is only one living and true God, and second, that the one God exists as Father, Son, and Holy Spirit. We will defer discussion of the Trinity to the next chapter. Here I am drawing attention to the tensions in the text of John's Gospel that require the explanation that Jesus was both God and man.

To feel the force of these tensions they need to be stated plainly in order. First, John clearly presents his message in fulfillment of the Old Testament, thus he has no intention of contradicting, changing, nullifying, or in any way denying the idea that there is one God (Deut. 6:4). At the same time, John affirms that the Word was God and was with God (John 1:1). The assertion in John 10:30 seems designed to resolve the apparent contradiction, as Jesus there asserts that he and the Father (two persons) are one.

The Father-Son language joins with the description of Jesus as the "only begotten" and as the recipient of "life in himself" from the Father to indicate that the Son is begotten of the Father. In order for the Son to be everything the Father is—that is, for the Word to be God (1:1) and for Jesus and the Father to be one (10:30)—the Son must be as eternal as the Father is. And John presents the Word being "in the beginning" (1:1) and having glory with the Father "before the world was" (17:5).

At the same time, John presents Jesus as the son of Mary, his mother, with brothers, offspring of David (e.g., 2:1; 7:3, 42; cf. 8:41, 48), born in the world and having recognizable age (see 8:57). The Word became flesh (1:14).[15] And John's Gospel attests to all the things Jesus accomplished on his first mission and promised

15. Cyril beautifully holds the humanity and divinity together: "I say that we must call him God made man, and that both the one and the other are this same reality, for he did not cease to be God when he became man, nor did he regard the economy as unacceptable by disdaining the limitations involved in the self-emptying." Cyril of Alexandria, *On the Unity of Christ*, trans. John Anthony McGuckin (Crestwood, NY: St. Vladimir's Seminary Press, 1995), 76.

to do on the second that we see in the C′ lines of the Athanasian Creed. Here I list them with representative references to these things being narrated or promised in John:

> Who suffered for our salvation (John 19:1–37)
>> Descended to the dead (i.e., was dead and buried; 19:38–42)
>>> Rose again on the third day from the dead (20:1–29)
>>>> He ascended into heaven (e.g., 3:13; 6:62; 7:34; 14:2)
>>>>> He sits on the right hand of the Father, God Almighty (16:28)
>>>>
>>>> From whence he shall come (14:3, 18)
>>>
>>> To judge the quick and the dead (5:21–22, 25–29)
>>
>> At whose coming all men shall rise again with their bodies (6:39–40)
>
> And shall give account for their own works (5:29)

These statements in the creed aptly summarize what John presents Jesus accomplishing and promising to accomplish at his return.

Reasonable Soul and Human Flesh

The creed affirms that Jesus had a reasonable, or rational, soul and human flesh. In support of his human rationality, we note that he asked real questions (e.g., 1:38; 2:3–4; 11:34). Jesus engaged in actual conversations with other human beings: Nicodemus, for example, and the Samaritan woman (John 3–4). Jesus everywhere makes logical arguments from Scripture, arguments that his followers and opponents fully understand (see esp. John 5 and 8 and the discussions of those chapters above). Jesus also evidences his reasonable soul in his displays of emotion, such as when he displayed zeal for the temple (2:17), when he wept over Lazarus (11:35), when he was troubled in soul at the prospect of his suffering (12:27), then similarly troubled in spirit (13:21), and note that he speaks of his will (5:30). As Cyril of Alexandria puts it, "The body which he united to himself was endowed with a rational soul, for the Word, who is God, would hardly neglect our finer part, the soul, and have regard only for the earthly body."[16]

The evidence that Jesus had human flesh abounds in John's Gospel. He was weary (4:6). He was thirsty (19:28). He died (19:33). He could be physically touched by others (20:27; cf. 1 John 1:1). He ate breakfast (John 21:10–15). Indeed, the Word became flesh (1:14).

Equal According to Godhead, Inferior According to Manhood

What I have marked above as the E and E′ lines of part 2 of the Athanasian Creed frame the central statement in line F. These two framing statements correspond to each other in that both mention Godhead and manhood, but aside from that formal correspondence, the E′ line really exposits the central statement about how though he is both God and man he is not two but one Christ. I will thus focus on the E line here and discuss the E′ line under the next subheading.

Here again it is worth stating necessary presuppositions, things we take for granted but that need to be explicitly stated. First, John believes the Old Testament, which affirms exclusive monotheism. Second, John is a coherent thinker with sufficient critical intellectual faculties to recognize manifest contradictions. Thus, third, when we encounter things that either look like they are not internally coherent or that may appear to contradict the Old Testament, we give John the benefit of the doubt and remain open to the possibility that he understands things in a way that accounts for what seems to be contradictory.

16. Cyril of Alexandria, *On the Unity of Christ*, 64.

With these considerations in mind, consider the following statements in John's Gospel:

- "The Word was with God, and the Word was God" (1:1);
- "He was also saying God was his own Father, making himself equal with God" (5:18);
- "I and the Father, one we are" (10:30); and
- "Because the Father is greater than I" (14:28).

Allow me to articulate some of the tensions created by these statements. First, if there is only one God, how can the Word also be God and with God (1:1)? Second, if there is only one God, how is it that Jesus can refer to himself and his Father, two persons, and maintain that they are one (10:30)? Third, if Jesus is equal with God (5:18), how can he say that the Father is greater than he is (14:28)? The first two of these we will explore in the next chapter on the Trinity. The third is directly addressed by the line of the creed under consideration here: "Equal to the Father, as touching his Godhead: and inferior to the Father, as touching his manhood."[17]

This simple statement preserves both the real divinity and the real humanity of Jesus, and it assigns the equality to the divinity and the inferiority to the humanity. If John thought about things in this way, there is no contradiction between Jesus being equal to the Father in John 5:18 and then calling the Father greater than himself in 14:28.[18] I submit that the Fourth Gospel shows John to have been a thinker sufficiently nuanced, coherent, searching, and profound to have recognized these tensions and only included them because in his framework of thought they created harmony rather than discord.

17. For further discussion of this issue, see Augustine, *The Trinity*, 74–90.

18. So also Cyril: "'He did not consider equality with God a thing to be grasped' but descended into a condition without glory insofar as he was revealed as man. This is why he said: 'The Father is greater than I,' even though he had the right to have exact equality with him in all things and to rejoice in the glory of the Godhead since he has existed with God eternally insofar as he is conceived as, and actually is, God." Cyril of Alexandria, *On the Unity of Christ*, 123.

One Christ

The central statement of the Athanasian Creed (the F line) states that though Jesus is two, God and man, he is one Christ. This statement is exposited (in the E′ line) with assertions that comport with Chalcedon: "No confusion, no change, no division, no separation."[19] The Athanasian Creed speaks to each of these points, as can be seen on the table below:

Chalcedon	Athanasian Creed
"No confusion"	"Not by confusion of substance"
"No change"	"Not by conversion of the Godhead into flesh, but by taking of the manhood into God"
"No division"	"Not two, but one Christ"
"No separation"	"One . . . by unity of person"

These statements affirm what John asserts in 1:14, "the Word became flesh." When the Word became flesh, he remained the Word. That the Word became flesh means that it was the Word who became a man. It is not the case that there was a separate human being with whom the Word somehow combined himself, nor is it the case that the Word left off being the Word and was somehow converted into being a human and was no longer God. He existed with God as the Word (1:1), and to his divine nature he added a human nature, assuming humanity. When this happened, the divine and the human substance, or natures, were not confused. The two natures remained truly what they were rather than becoming a third nature unlike either of the other two. In his one person Jesus unites the two natures.

Thus in the Gospel of John we are not confronted with two figures, something like a human Jesus and a divine Christ, the one acting like a mere mortal man, the other like God. Rather, in John's Gospel we encounter one person, Jesus of Nazareth, and

19. See Philip Schaff, *The Creeds of Christendom*, vol. 2, *The Greek and Latin Creeds, with Translations* (New York: Harper & Brothers, 1919), 62–63.

John asserts of him that he is the divine Word made flesh and the man from Nazareth born of Mary. Herman Bavinck summarizes the evidence well: "Every moment in Scripture, divine as well as human predicates are attributed to the same personal subject: divine and human existence, omnipresence and [geographical] limitation, eternity and time, creative omnipotence and creaturely weakness. What else is this but the church's doctrine of the two natures united in one person?"[20]

Conclusion

I need corrective lenses to sharpen my perception of objects more than a short distance away. These lenses do not distort my vision but improve it. The orthodox understanding of the incarnation articulated in the Athanasian Creed functions the same way my spectacles do, sharpening perception of what is actually there. If I refuse to put on my glasses, the distant objects are still there, but I do not see them in detail. For too long academic study of the Bible has, in essence, encouraged students and professors to try to see without the prescription lenses that would enable them to understand what their unaided eyes only vaguely perceive. "In order to do justice to all the scriptural data concerning the person of Christ, [Christian] theology arrived gradually at the two-natures doctrine. It did not put this doctrine forward as a hypothesis, nor did it intend it as an explanation of the mystery of Christ's person. In it, it only summed up, without mutilation and diminution, the whole scriptural doctrine of Christ and thereby maintained it against the errors that cropped up both to the left and to the right."[21]

20. Bavinck, *Reformed Dogmatics*, 3:299.
21. Bavinck, *Reformed Dogmatics*, 3:301.

Questions for Reflection and Discussion

1. As you read the Gospel of John, do you do so on the assumption that John has a full understanding of all that would come to be articulated in the statement on the incarnation in the Athanasian Creed?
2. Are you part of a church that regularly recites the Apostles', Nicene, and Athanasian Creeds? If so, has the regular recitation led to memorization? If not, can you think of a way to incorporate the creeds into your personal life so that you become thoroughly familiar with their language, phrasing, and teaching?

Suggested Reading

Irons, Charles Lee. "A Lexical Defense of the Johannine 'Only Begotten.'" In *Retrieving Eternal Generation*, edited by Fred Sanders and Scott R. Swain. Grand Rapids: Zondervan, 2017.

Jamieson, R. B. *The Paradox of Sonship: Christology in the Epistle to the Hebrews*. Studies in Christian Doctrine and Scripture. Downers Grove, IL: InterVarsity, 2021.

Rowe, C. Kavin. *Early Narrative Christology: The Lord in the Gospel of Luke*. Grand Rapids: Baker Academic, 2009.

Yeago, David S. "The New Testament and the Nicene Dogma: A Contribution to the Recovery of Theological Exegesis." *Sewanee Theological Review* 45 (2002): 371–84.

10

THE TRINITY IN JOHN'S GOSPEL

> At one and the same time—this is the wonder—
> as Man He was living a human life,
> and as Word He was sustaining the life of the universe,
> and as Son He was in constant union with the Father.
>
> —Athanasius, *On the Incarnation* §18[1]

In the previous chapter we noted the tensions created by the juxtaposition of statements like Deuteronomy 6:4 and Isaiah 42:8 with statements like John 10:30 and 17:5. Consider these in conjunction with one another:

- "Hear O Israel, Yahweh our God, Yahweh is one" (Deut. 6:4).
- "I am Yahweh. That is my name. My glory to another I will not give" (Isa. 42:8).

1. Athanasius, *On the Incarnation: De Incarnatione Verbi Dei* (Crestwood, NY: St. Vladimir's Seminary Press, 1998), 45.

- "I and the Father, one we are" (John 10:30).
- "And now, glorify me, Father, with yourself with the glory that I had with you before the world was" (John 17:5).

These could be dismissed as contradictions, but that conclusion would be too hasty and would fail to consider the way that, on the one hand, the New Testament everywhere affirms the authority of the Old (cf., e.g., John 10:35, "The Scripture cannot be broken"),[2] and on the other, the New Testament's revelations about Christ and the Spirit explain "unusual phenomena" from the Old Testament that point to a plurality within the one God. To what do I refer? From just the first chapter of Genesis, we see God create in verse 1, the Spirit of God hovering over the waters in verse 2, and then God speaks in the first person plural in verse 26, "Let us make." When he then creates man in his own image and likeness, he is not said to have made a single person but two, a male and a female, in verse 27.

Another curious feature of the presentation of God in Genesis is the way that in 19:24 we read, "And Yahweh caused to rain upon Sodom and upon Gomorrah brimstone and fire from Yahweh from the heavens." It seems that there are two Yahwehs in the verse—one who stands on earth, having visited Abraham and gone on to Sodom (Gen. 18:1–33), the other in the heavens, from whom fire and brimstone rain down. I am not suggesting that this is a Christophany. Augustine has argued convincingly that we should understand Yahweh as sending created angels as his representatives,[3] and we should not diminish the incarnation by suggesting it took place in some partial way before the Word became flesh.[4]

2. Rightly Kavin Rowe: "The writers of the New Testament presupposed the authority of the Old Testament and made explicit use of the theological grammar that undergirds the Old Testament's language about the one God." C. Kavin Rowe, "Biblical Pressure and Trinitarian Hermeneutics," *Pro Ecclesia* 11 (2002): 299.

3. Augustine, *The Trinity*, in *The Works of Saint Augustine: A Translation for the 21st Century*, trans. Edmund Hill (Brooklyn, NY: New City, 1991), 112, 140–46.

4. Against Christophanies, see also Andrew S. Malone, *Knowing Jesus in the Old Testament? A Fresh Look at Christophanies* (Downers Grove, IL: InterVarsity, 2015).

I am suggesting that what Jesus says in John 10:30 both affirms Deuteronomy 6:4 and explains these realities from the Old Testament. Fred Sanders helpfully explains:

> In the time period documented by the Old Testament, God was triune but was not actively revealing that triunity to his covenant people. Whatever adumbrations may be found in the text, no revelations are to be sought there. . . . For this reason, it is best not to press the Old Testament to make it yield Trinitarian revelation. The text of the Old Testament and the trajectory of its events do generate a host of unusual phenomena that need to be accounted for. They are best accounted for by Trinitarian theology as it throws a light backward from the New Testament to the Old.[5]

The claim of this chapter is that the revelation of Jesus and the Spirit as God with the Father in John's Gospel thus pulls back the curtain on the backstory that provides the most satisfying understanding of the Old Testament's mysteries. John's trinitarian Gospel supplies its audience with the intellectually coherent resolution and fulfillment that students of the Old Testament need. Rowe states the matter plainly when he writes, "To interpret the Bible in light of the doctrine of the Trinity does not, therefore, distort its basic content but penetrates to its core with respect to the reality of the divine identity, the living God outside of the text known truly by Israel and fully in Jesus Christ."[6]

5. Sanders, *The Triune God*, New Studies in Dogmatics (Grand Rapids: Zondervan, 2016), 22.

6. Rowe, "Biblical Pressure and Trinitarian Hermeneutics," 311. A few pages earlier (308) in the same essay he writes,

> The ontological judgments of the early ecumenical Creeds were the only satisfying and indeed logical outcome of the claims of the New Testament read together with the Old. That is to say, for a Christian faith that upholds the unity of the Bible and the continuing authority of the Old Testament, the one God is Trinity in himself, affirmed on the basis of his economic expression. There is no other way to justify the claims about and worship of the fully human Jesus Christ within an Old Testament framework. It is likewise with the Spirit: given the authority of the Old Testament, to

In an effort to demonstrate these claims, the remainder of this chapter will first summarize the chiastic structure of part 1 of the Athanasian Creed on the Trinity. We will provide the text of this part of the creed formatted as a chiasm, then, following Sanders again,[7] crystallize its "leading ideas" and explain these from what John shows and tells about the Father, Son, and Holy Spirit.

Part 1 of the Athanasian Creed: The Trinity

As we did for part 2 on the incarnation in the previous chapter, we can summarize the message of corresponding sections of part 1 of the Athanasian Creed before considering how it encapsulates John's teaching. Both parts of the creed begin and end by stating that those who would be saved must believe the content of these assertions (A and A′). The second and second-to-last statements (B and B′) connect right faith to true worship, affirming that the one God is worshiped in Trinity and Trinity in unity. In the C and C′ lines, third and third to last, the singularity of the divine persons, Father, Son, and Spirit, is affirmed alongside their equality and eternality as God. Fourth and fourth to last we have first, in the D line, affirmation of the undivided substance of Father, Son, and Spirit, and second, in the D′ line, confession of the eternal relations of origin. At the center of this chiastic structure are two four-part statements, both affirming that the three persons are the one God in the E and E′ sections, describing the members of the Godhead as uncreated, unbounded, and unlimited by time on the one hand, and on the other as almighty, divine, and Lord.

recognize the "personhood" of the Spirit in coordination with the claims of the New Testament regarding the Spirit's inseparability from Jesus Christ in worship and in presence is to affirm that the Spirit, too, is of the "same essence" as the Father and the Son. For the church to turn its back upon the Creeds is to turn its back upon the Old Testament.

7. Fred Sanders, "Biblical Grounding for the Christology of the Councils," *Criswell Theological Review* 13 (2015): 93.

The chiastic structure of part 1 of the Athanasian Creed can be depicted as follows (bold font, italics, and underlining mark corresponding words and phrases):

A Whoever desires to be saved must above all hold to the true Christian faith. Anyone who does not keep it whole and unbroken will doubtless perish eternally. And the true Christian faith is this:

B That **we worship one God in Trinity and Trinity in unity**, neither confounding the persons nor dividing the substance.

C For there is one Person of the Father, another of the Son, and another of the Holy Spirit. But the Godhead of the Father, of the Son, and of the Holy Spirit, is all one: the Glory *equal*, the Majesty *co-eternal*.

D Such as the Father is, such is the Son, and such is the Holy Spirit.

E The Father uncreated, the Son uncreated, and the Holy Spirit uncreated. The Father incomprehensible, the Son incomprehensible, and the Holy Spirit incomprehensible. The Father eternal, the Son eternal, and the Holy Spirit eternal. And yet they are not three eternals: but one eternal. As also there are not three incomprehensibles, nor three uncreated, but one uncreated, and one incomprehensible.

E′ So likewise the Father is Almighty, the Son Almighty, and the Holy Spirit Almighty. And yet they are not three Almighties: but one Almighty. So the Father is God, the Son is God, and the Holy Spirit is God. And yet they are not three Gods, but one God. So likewise the

Father is Lord, the Son Lord, and the Holy Spirit Lord. And yet not three Lords, but one Lord. For just as we are compelled by the Christian verity to acknowledge every Person by himself to be God and Lord, so are we forbidden by the true Christian faith to say there be three Gods, or three Lords.

D′ The Father is made of none: neither created nor begotten. The Son is of the Father alone: not made, nor created, but begotten. The Holy Spirit is of the Father and of the Son: neither made, nor created, nor begotten, but proceeding.

C′ So there is one Father, not three Fathers; one Son, not three Sons; one Holy Spirit, not three Holy Spirits. And in this Trinity none is afore or after another, none is greater or less than another, but the whole three persons are *co-eternal* together and *co-equal*.

B′ So that in all things, as is aforesaid: the unity in Trinity, and the Trinity in unity is to be worshipped.

A′ Any therefore that will be saved must thus think of the Trinity.

As with part 2 in the previous chapter, so with part 1 we can summarize these statements as follows:

Necessary belief

Worship of the Triune God

Distinct persons, Godhead equal and eternal

Undivided substance

Father, Son, and Spirit are uncreated, infinite, and eternal

Not three divine natures but one

Father, Son, and Spirit are almighty, divine, and Lord

Not three Lord Gods but one

Eternal relations of origin

Distinct persons, Trinity eternal and equal

Worship of the Triune God

Necessary belief

Working from the outer rings (necessary belief) down (through worship and distinct persons, etc.) to the center (three persons one God), we can summarize the leading ideas of part 1 of the creed on the Trinity with the following bullet points, which in turn will become the subheads for discussion of John's teaching on these points:

- Necessary belief
- Worship
- Distinct persons equal and eternal
- Undivided substance with eternal relations of origin
- Three persons one God

Necessary Belief

The statements that provide the outer frame for the Trinity section, part 1, of the Athanasian Creed, affirm that those who would be saved must keep what this document asserts in its entirety, giving way at no part: "Whole and unbroken" (A line). John presents Jesus telling his disciples that the world cannot receive the Spirit he will send to them because it neither sees him nor knows him, but they know him because he dwells with them and will be in them (John 14:17). To believe the assertions of the Athanasian Creed is to understand that Jesus and the Spirit are both God, distinguishable and inseparable, and therefore by virtue of being with Jesus they have been with the Spirit, who, after all, came down upon Jesus to remain (1:29–34). Just as Jesus came in fulfillment of the temple and was filled with the Spirit, so he will send his disciples as he was sent: in fulfillment of the temple and filled with the Spirit (20:21–23).

Understanding that the three persons of the Godhead are one gives us a framework for interpreting what Jesus goes on to say in John 14:20–21: "In that day you will know that I am in my Father; and you are in me, and I in you. The one who has my commandments and keeps them, he is the one who loves me. And the one who loves me will be loved by my Father, and I will love him and manifest myself to him." Jesus and the Father are in one another (14:20a) because they are of one "substance" (or "essence" or "nature"). As Jesus says in John 10:30, "I and the Father, one we are." The disciples will receive the indwelling Spirit (14:17b); and thereby they will be in Jesus, and he will be in them (14:20b). The indwelling Spirit will likewise produce love for Jesus that results in desire to do what he commands (14:21a), resulting in further communion with God (14:21b). As Rowe has written, "The ontological judgments of the early ecumenical Creeds were the only satisfying and indeed logical outcome of the claims of the New Testament."[8]

John presents Jesus asserting himself as the way, the truth, and the life, and further, that no one comes to the Father except through him (14:6). The only way to go to the Father through Jesus is to believe what Jesus taught. The conclusions articulated in statements like the Athanasian Creed are not deviations from that message but restatements that enable it to be more fully understood. The A′ line of part 1 of the Athanasian Creed serves as an apt paraphrase of John 14:6, clarifying the meaning of that verse with technical terminology that presents in shorthand fashion what the broader narrative implies: "Any therefore that will be saved must thus think of the Trinity."

8. Rowe, "Biblical Pressure and Trinitarian Hermeneutics," 308.

Worship

The second and second-to-last statements (B and B′) of this part of the creed both affirm that to know God is to worship him. Conversely, not to know God as Trinity is not to know him as he is. Those who do not know God worship something, but what they worship is not God as he is revealed in the Bible. True worship requires right faith (cf. 4:20–24).

God reveals himself in his triune glory in the New Testament to provoke faith, wonder, admiration, praise, and exultant gratitude (cf. 1:14, 18; 2:11; 4:39, 53, etc.). The creeds were not produced by stale hearts preoccupied with irrelevant and useless metaphysical speculation divorced from the biblical text. Rather, the biblical text itself exerts "pressure" (to use the term in the title of Rowe's essay) on those who ponder its implications, pushing them to understand and account for the things stated in the text. As Cyril of Alexandria insisted, "We follow the mind of the divinely inspired writers."[9] Those who love God and want to please him seek to honor him by bringing their thoughts into line with the Scriptures, and thus the statements at beginning and end of this part of the creed that this document is about *worshiping* the one God in Trinity and Trinity in unity.

The second statement in the B line of part 1 asserts the big idea exposited throughout the creed's statements on the Trinity: "Neither confounding the persons nor dividing the substance." This means that Father, Son, and Spirit are not mixed up with one another, as though the Father might be equated or interchanged with the Son or Spirit and vice versa. These three are distinct, unconfounded, and yet the substance, their divine nature or essence, is the same, undivided. The Father is not the Son or the Spirit; the

9. Cyril of Alexandria, *On the Unity of Christ*, trans. John Anthony McGuckin (Crestwood, NY: St. Vladimir's Seminary Press, 1995), 89. A few pages later Cyril asserts, "And the preaching of those who were divinely inspired does not lie" (91).

Son is not the Father or the Spirit; the Spirit is not the Father or the Son; and at the same time Father, Son, and Spirit are the one God.

The revelation of glory provokes worship. Glory, distinction in personhood, and the undivided substance of the Godhead can be seen together in the Gospel of John. When the time comes, Jesus says in John 12:28, "Father, glorify your name." The Father then answers in 12:29, "I have glorified, and again I will glorify." In the immediate context Jesus said, "The hour has come that the Son of Man might be glorified" (12:23). When the Son of Man is glorified the Father will be glorifying his own name because *as Lord* (the titular translation of Yahweh) Jesus bears the name of the Father. As Rowe has observed, "The Creator of the world and Redeemer of Israel had a proper name and had revealed this name to Israel. In Hebrew the name is YHWH. . . . It is safe to say that the writers of the New Testament understood this name in Greek as *kyrios*."[10] The Father is not being confused with the Son, and yet the Father is glorifying himself as the Son is glorified. And this glory results in worship, as can be seen in John 12:32, "And I, if I am lifted up from the earth, will draw all men to myself" (cf. also 4:23–24).

The words of Jesus in John 16:14 show that the Spirit, unconfused person and undivided substance, likewise glorifies: "He will glorify me, because he will take from what is mine and proclaim it to you." And in this context we do well to recall Yahweh's assertion in Isaiah 42:8, that he is Yahweh, that is his name, and his glory he gives to no other.

The B line near the creed's beginning states the thesis, "neither confounding the persons nor dividing the substance." The body of the creed then exposits that thesis, and near the end its message is summarized in the B′ line's statement "so that in all things, as is aforesaid . . ." demonstrating that the worship of the unity in Trinity and the Trinity in unity, unconfounded persons

10. Rowe, "Biblical Pressure and Trinitarian Hermeneutics," 301.

and undivided substance, constitutes the big idea of part 1 of the Athanasian Creed.

Distinct Persons Equal and Eternal

The equality and eternality of the unconfounded persons of undivided substance receives further explanation in the C and C′ lines of part 1 of the creed. In the C line, Father, Son, and Spirit are listed as three distinct persons, then a disjunctive adverb ("but") transitions to the affirmation that the three of them share the same Godhead, equal in glory and coeternal in majesty. This articulates what we see in the opening statement of the Gospel of John, when the Word is described as being both God and with God, and as having been so "in the beginning" (1:1–2). Prior to the foundation of the world (see "all things were made through him" in 1:3), with the rotation of the earth to constitute moments, hours, and days, with the orbiting moon to mark months, and with the earth circling the sun to mark years (cf. Gen. 1:14), the Word was there with the Father, distinct in person, coeternal in majesty.

Similarly, the Son sends the distinct person of the Spirit from the Father (John 15:26a), who proceeds from the Father to bear witness to the Son (15:26b). This Spirit of God was there at the beginning when all was made (Gen. 1:2), and in him Christ remains with his people even when he returns to the Father (John 14:15–21). Indeed, by means of the indwelling Spirit, the Father and the Son make their home with the disciples of Jesus (14:23). To be indwelled by the Spirit is to be indwelled by Father and Son, for though they are distinct persons, they are one God. As Cyril puts it, "The fullness of the consubstantial Trinity dwells within us through the Spirit."[11] The eternality of the Spirit is attested by his presence at creation in the beginning (Gen. 1:2) and affirmed when Jesus tells his disciples that the Spirit will be with them *forever* (John 14:16).

11. Cyril of Alexandria, *On the Unity of Christ*, 96.

The affirmations of the C line are matched by the denials of the C′ line. There are not three Fathers, there are not three Sons, and there are not three Spirits. This time a conjunctive adverb ("and"; cf. the "but" in C) stands in the center of the line as the statement moves to assert that no member of the Trinity is before or after another, that none is greater or less than another (see the discussion of John 14:28 in the previous chapter, for which the creed accounts), but that the three are coeternal and coequal.

Undivided Substance with Eternal Relations of Origin

The D line of part 1 of the creed affirms that what the Father is the Son is, and the same holds for the Holy Spirit. In John's Gospel, Jesus asserts himself as "the way, the truth, and the life" (14:6). He is the only begotten of the Father, full of grace and truth (1:14), and truth is characteristic of God, as Yahweh declared himself in Exodus 34:6–7, "abounding in steadfast love and truth." Cyril of Alexandria argues, "For whatever is not a natural property, but is given by someone else as an external addition, is not the property of the one who receives it, but of the one who bestows it as a gift. But if this were so how could he possibly say 'I am the truth' (Jn 14:6) if there is nothing true about him?"[12] Similarly, the Spirit is "the Spirit of truth" (John 14:17), whom the Father will send in the name of Jesus (14:26), who will lead the disciples into all truth (16:13), by taking from what belongs to the Father and Jesus and declaring it to the disciples (16:14–15). The same kinds of observations can be made about life, which the Father granted Jesus to have in himself (5:26), so that life is in him (1:4). At the same time, Jesus can assert, "The Spirit is the one who gives life" (6:63).

The substance is not divided.

The matching D′ section of the creed teaches how the persons are to be distinguished from one another in explicitly biblical, indeed Johannine, categories. No member of the Godhead, Father,

12. Cyril of Alexandria, *On the Unity of Christ*, 90.

Son, or Spirit, is either made or created. God created the world and was not made or created by anything or anyone else. This restates the way that John 1:3 asserts, "All things through him became, and apart from him became not even one that became." The Father is begotten of none, but the Son is begotten of the Father, a truth articulated by the Son being described as the "only begotten" (1:14, 18; 3:16, 18), by him receiving life in himself from the Father (5:26), and by him being the light of the world, the emanating glory of the Father (e.g., 1:4–5, 9, 14; 3:19; 8:12).[13] The Son is described as being "of the Father alone" because there is no mention of the Spirit being involved in the Son being begotten from the Father. The Spirit, by contrast, is "of the Father and of the Son" because both the Father and the Son are involved in the sending of the Spirit (14:26; 15:26a; 16:7), who was not begotten but who "proceeds" from the Father and the Son (15:26b). Gregory of Nazianzus explains, "Insofar as he proceeds from the Father, he is no creature; inasmuch as he is not begotten, he is no Son; and to the extent that procession is the mean between ingeneracy and generacy, he is God."[14] And Augustine helpfully spells out the implications of what John says about Father, Son, and Spirit: "The Father has begotten the Son, and therefore he who is the Father is

13. Commenting on Heb. 1:3, R. B. Jamieson observes, "The one who subsists as the outflow of God's glory and impress of his essence is himself God by nature. However, both predicates also imply derivation, 'from-ness': light shines from a source; an impress derives from its mold. Hence these predicates assert both identity with God and relation to God, both sameness and distinction." R. B. Jamieson, *The Paradox of Sonship: Christology in the Epistle to the Hebrews*, Studies in Christian Doctrine and Scripture (Downers Grove, IL: InterVarsity, 2021), 69–70.

14. Gregory of Nazianzus, *On God and Christ: Five Theological Orations and Two Letters to Cledonius*, trans. Frederick Williams and Lionel R. Wickham, Popular Patristics Series (Crestwood, NY: St. Vladimir's Seminary Press, 2002), 122. Gregory continues, "Thus God escapes your syllogistic toils and shows himself stronger than your exclusive alternatives. What, then, is 'proceeding'? You explain the ingeneracy of the Father and I will give you a biological account of the Son's begetting and the Spirit's proceeding—and let us go mad the pair of us for prying into God's secrets. What competence have we here?"

not the Son; and the Son is begotten by the Father, and therefore he who is the Son is not the Father; and the Holy Spirit is neither the Father nor the Son, but only the Spirit of the Father and of the Son, himself coequal to the Father and the Son, and belonging to the threefold unity."[15]

The persons are not confounded.

The statements in the D and D′ lines of part 1 of the Athanasian Creed articulate the eternal relations of origin of the undivided substance of the Triune God. John's Gospel reveals that the Son is begotten of the Father and that the Spirit proceeds from the Father and the Son. The Bible says nothing about the Father's origin, and where the Bible is silent the creed is too, simply stating, "The Father is made of none: neither created nor begotten." The creed summarizes what John's Gospel says about the distinct descriptions of the relations of origin of the members of the Godhead in eternity past.

Three Persons One God

When we arrive at the E and E′ lines of part 1 of the Athanasian Creed, we have come to its two fourfold central statements. These have a clear pattern and rhythm. In the first, Father, Son, and Spirit are affirmed as uncreated, incomprehensible (in the sense of boundless), and eternal, and then the creed goes back through the descriptors in reverse order to say that there are not three eternals but one, not three incomprehensibles but one, and not three uncreated but one. The point is to affirm that all three are truly everything God is but also to deny that this means there are three gods. The one God exists as three persons, and each of the three persons is everything God is.

In the second the pattern is slightly modified so that the denial that there are three different gods comes at the end of each of the affirmations, rather than the denials being grouped together after

15. Augustine, *The Trinity*, 69.

the affirmations as in the first. Thus Father, Son, and Spirit are affirmed as being almighty, God, and Lord, and yet this does not mean there are three almighties, three gods, or three lords. There is one almighty, one God, and one Lord, and Father, Son, and Spirit are each everything God is: almighty, God, and Lord.

The New Testament manifestly affirms that Father, Son, and Spirit are God, and the creed assumes that the authors of the New Testament have a coherent idea of what that entails. If Father, Son, and Spirit are one God, if the Father as creator is uncreated, and if the Father created through the Word (John 1:3), then the Word begotten of the Father is also uncreated. Though the text does not explicitly state that the Spirit is likewise uncreated, if he is God he must be.[16] The situation is similar with "incomprehensibility" in the sense of "unbounded," an aspect of which is communicated when the Word is described as the light shining in the darkness that the darkness has not "overcome" or "comprehended," in the sense that the darkness has not "overtaken" the light (1:5).[17] Here again, if this is true of the Word, it must also be true of the Father and the Spirit.

16. Hill explains in his introduction to Augustine's *On the Trinity*: "If the Son and the Holy Spirit are truly God, they have (or rather are) all the attributes that belong to the Father, and they do (or rather are) all the acts which the Father does (is)" (45).

17. Athanasius reflects as follows on what it means for Christ to be simultaneously human and divine, and as God for him to be incomprehensibly unbounded:

> The Word was not hedged in by His body, nor did His presence in the body prevent His being present elsewhere as well. When He moved His body He did not cease also to direct the universe by His Mind and might. No. The marvelous truth is, that being the Word, so far from being Himself contained by anything, He actually contained all things Himself. In creation He is present everywhere, yet is distinct in being from it; ordering, directing, giving life to all, containing all, yet is He Himself the Uncontained, existing solely in His Father. As with the whole, so also is it with the part. Existing in a human body, to which He Himself gives life, He is still Source of life to all the universe, present in every part of it, yet outside the whole; and He is revealed both through the works of His body and through His activity in the world. (Athanasius, *On the Incarnation* §17, 45)

We have commented on the eternality of the Spirit above. With regard to the Father and the Son, we can note that they were "in the beginning" (John 1:1), that Jesus speaks of having glory with the Father before the world was (17:5), and that all the language of Jesus being "sent" from the Father and "returning to where he was before" (e.g., 6:57, 62; 7:28–29, 33; 8:14; 10:36) points to Father and Son having enjoyed and enjoying never-beginning and never-ending communion. Thus the Son asserts his oneness with the Father (10:30) and prays for his disciples to be unified (17:22b).

The oneness asserted in John 10:30, "I and the Father are one" (ESV), also undergirds the creed's affirmation that there are not three eternals, three incomprehensibles, and three uncreated but only the one living and true God.

The creed next affirms that Father, Son, and Spirit are almighty, God, and Lord in the one nature shared by the three persons. We see the Son's almighty power in John when Jesus turns water to wine (2:1–12) and raises Lazarus from the dead (11:43–44). We see the Spirit's almighty power when Jesus asserts that he is the one who gives life (6:63). And Jesus affirms that the Father is greater than all, whom no one can overcome (10:29), immediately after asserting that no one can take his sheep from him (10:28), immediately before asserting his oneness with the Father (10:30), which implies that he shares the status of being "greater than all" (10:29).

That "they are not three Almighties: but one Almighty" entails the idea that no member of the Godhead will be excluded from any exercise of the power of the one God (inseparable operations).[18] In his treatise *On the Holy Spirit* Basil of Caesarea interprets the Gospel of John on just this point: "The work of the Father is not separate or distinct from the work of the Son; whatever the Son 'sees the Father doing . . . that the Son does likewise' [John 5:19]. . . . He shines forth from the Father, and accomplishes

18. Thanks are due to my friend, fellow elder, and faculty colleague Kyle Claunch for helping me to think through this issue.

everything according to His Parent's plan. He is not different in essence, nor is He different in power from His Father, and if their power is equal, then their works are the same."[19]

As for Father, Son, and Spirit being God, all three are depicted in John's Gospel as being able to do what only God can.[20] On the matter of Father, Son, and Spirit being "Lord," it may be the case that the creed is using the term "Lord" as the titular translation of the divine name, Yahweh. In John's Gospel, the response of Thomas in 20:28, "My Lord and my God!" (ESV) likely carries this connotation.[21] If Thomas is going to identify Jesus as his God, this would naturally correspond to Thomas identifying Jesus with Yahweh. If the Father sends the Spirit in Jesus' name (14:26), and if Jesus bears the name Yahweh, then the Spirit comes in the name of Yahweh. This understanding of what God reveals of himself as Father, Son, and Spirit, three persons who bear the one name, informs the baptismal instructions in Matthew 28:19, "baptizing them in the name of the Father and of the Son and of the Holy Spirit" (ESV), and also Paul's comment in 2 Corinthians 3:17, "Now the Lord is the Spirit, and where the Spirit of the Lord is, freedom" (cf. John 8:34–36).[22]

In addition to the idea that Father, Son, and Spirit are "Lord" in the sense that they are Yahweh, the creed likely means to attribute

19. Basil of Caesarea, *On the Holy Spirit*, trans. David Anderson (Crestwood, NY: St. Vladimir's Seminary Press, 1980), 39.

20. See table 2, "Actions of God in John," which details "actions common to Father, Son, and Spirit"; "actions common to Father and Son"; and "actions common to Son and Spirit," in James M. Hamilton Jr., *God's Indwelling Presence: The Holy Spirit in the Old and New Testaments*, NAC Studies in Bible and Theology (Nashville: B&H, 2006), 56. These actions include things like giving life, proclaiming the future, indwelling believers, etc.

21. Rowe notes the similarity in phrasing between the Greek translation of Ps. 34:23–24 (ὁ θεός μου καὶ ὁ κύριός μου and κύριε ὁ θεός μου) and John 20:28 (ὁ κύριός μου καὶ ὁ θεός μου). Rowe, "Biblical Pressure and Trinitarian Hermeneutics," 302.

22. Rowe writes, "There is a common (and in many ways understandable) assumption that YHWH, the God of the Old Testament, is the Father *only*. This assumption, however, will not stand under exegetical scrutiny. The New Testament texts never identify the Father as the Son or vice-versa, but they do give the divine name *kyrios* (= YHWH) to both the Father and the Son." Rowe, "Biblical Pressure and Trinitarian Hermeneutics," 303.

lordship in the sense of *authority* equally to Father, Son, and Spirit as God. The Son begotten of the Father has life in himself (5:26) and can thereby raise the dead, and he also received from the Father authority to lay down his life and take it up again (10:18). As with the grant of life in himself, the Son must have received this authority from the Father always, otherwise there would have been a time when he was not what the Father is. John pushes his audience to such conclusions by asserting things like "the Word was with God, and the Word was God" (1:1 ESV), by drawing out the implications of what Jesus said when he was "making himself equal with God" (5:18 ESV), and by depicting Jesus asserting of himself, "I and the Father are one" (10:30 ESV). Along these lines, the Father has granted all that belongs to him to the Son: "All that the Father has is mine" (16:15 ESV). And the Father and Son have likewise granted to the Spirit who proceeds from them authority over all that belongs to them: "He will take from what is mine and declare it to you" (16:14b). What John has written in his Gospel demands the conclusion that Father, Son, and Spirit are Lord, and yet not three lords but one Lord.

That there are "not three Lords, but one Lord" means that there is a single divine will exercised by the three persons of the Godhead. I cannot improve upon the words of Basil of Caesarea, who comments as follows on a string of texts in John's Gospel:

> When He says, "I have not spoken on my own authority," [John 12:49] and "As the Father has said unto me, so I speak" [12:50] and "the word which you hear is not mine but the Father's who sent me" [14:24] and "I do as the Father has commanded me," [14:31] He does not use language of this kind because He is incapable of his own choice, or is lawless, or has to wait for a prearranged signal. He wants to make it clear that His will is indissolubly united to the Father. We must not think that what He calls a "commandment" [10:18] is an imperious order delivered by word of mouth by which the Father gives orders to His Son, as He would to a subordinate, telling Him what He should do. Instead, let us think

> in terms worthy of the Godhead, and realize that there is a transmission of will, like the reflection of an object in a mirror, which reaches from Father to Son without passage of time. "The Father loves the Son, and shows Him all that He Himself is doing." [5:20] Everything the Father has also belongs to the Son; He does not acquire it little by little, but has it all at once.[23]

Conclusion

Throughout this book we have seen that in his Gospel John presents Jesus as the one who brings about the fulfillment of the Old Testament. This reality is no less true of the reflections on the incarnation and the Trinity in these final two chapters, for as Kavin Rowe has written, "The relation of God the Father, Jesus Christ, and the Spirit as well as the relation of Jesus' divinity and humanity had to be specified in terms consistent with the most fundamental theological thrust of the Old Testament, that of the unity and singularity of the one Creator God and the directives for exclusive worship that were inextricably bound with this God's identity."[24] This has been a book exploring the theology of John's Gospel, and by "theology" I mean "biblical theology," which I understand to be the attempt to understand and embrace the interpretive perspective of the biblical authors. Their interpretive perspective starts with their master story, and John's master story begins in eternity past and extends into eternity future, with redemptive history as the true story of the whole world in between. From what the biblical authors teach about the master story, we derive truths, symbols, ethics, and liturgy. The term "liturgy" refers to what we do in worship, and the Athanasian Creed reflects what Christians through time and across space have done: "We worship one God in Trinity

23. Basil of Caesarea, *On the Holy Spirit*, 40.
24. Rowe, "Biblical Pressure and Trinitarian Hermeneutics," 307.

and Trinity in unity." We praise God the Father through the Son by the Spirit.

World without end. Amen.

Questions for Reflection and Discussion

1. When you think of worship, of knowing God, of abiding in Christ, and of walking in the Spirit, where does the contemplation of God as triune fit?
2. Given that Deuteronomy 6:5 calls us to love the Lord with all we are all the time, none of us think about God enough, and none of us contemplate the Trinity enough. What steps can we take, habits can we form, disciplines can we practice to address our deficiency?

Suggested Reading

Hamilton, James M., Jr. "The Chiastic Structure of the Athanasian Creed." *Journal of the Evangelical Theological Society* 66 (2023): 279–300.

Rowe, C. Kavin. "Biblical Pressure and Trinitarian Hermeneutics." *Pro Ecclesia* 11 (2002): 295–312.

Rowe, C. Kavin. "Luke and the Trinity: An Essay in Ecclesial Biblical Theology." *Scottish Journal of Theology* 56 (2003): 1–26.

Sanders, Fred. "Biblical Grounding for the Christology of the Councils." *Criswell Theological Review* 13 (2015): 93–104.

ACKNOWLEDGMENTS

Praise and thanks, first and foremost, always to the Father through the Son by the Spirit, and in this case for inspiring John the son of Zebedee to write the Gospel that bears his name.

I also want to thank past and present PhD students who read this book closely and offered invaluable feedback: Wenya Yang, Jonny Atkinson, Greg Birdwell, Tom Sculthorpe, and Laurens Pruis. Your friendship and kindness are deeply appreciated.

I once read a writer (I forget who or where, but now I'm quoting his line) who said this about his wife: Without her I couldn't write a sentence.

I wish to express my gratitude to Jesse Myers, Eddie LaRow, Amy Nemecek, and the team at Baker for the investment they've made in this project. This book would exist apart from you, but only as a Word document in my saved files. Thank you.

The trustees and administration at The Southern Baptist Theological Seminary (SBTS) make it possible for members of the faculty like myself to research and write, and the elders and the members of Kenwood Baptist Church at Victory Memorial pray and support and build together an atmosphere of spiritual health. I'm not putting Kenwood and SBTS in the place of God by this chiastic structure (!), but both are used of God to make books like this possible. Heartfelt thanks.

JAMES M. HAMILTON JR., PhD, is professor of biblical theology at The Southern Baptist Theological Seminary and senior pastor of Kenwood Baptist Church in Louisville, Kentucky. He is the author of several books, most recently *Typology* and a two-volume commentary on Psalms in the Evangelical Biblical Theology Commentary Series.